Wildflower

Wildflower

❧

DREW BARRYMORE

DUTTON
— est. 1852 —

B BARRYMORE

DUTTON
— est. 1852 —

An imprint of Penguin Random House LLC
375 Hudson Street
New York, New York 10014

LIBRARY OF CONGRESS CATALOGING-IN-PUBLICATION DATA
Barrymore, Drew.
Wildflower / Drew Barrymore.
pages cm
ISBN 978-1-101-98379-9 (hardback)—ISBN 978-1-101-98380-5 (ebook) 1. Barrymore, Drew.
2. Actors—United States—Biography. I. Title.
PN2287.B29A3 2015
791.4302'8092—dc23
[B]
2015028835

Printed in the United States of America
1 3 5 7 9 10 8 6 4 2

Set in Carre Noir Std
Designed by Alissa Rose Theodor

To my friend family
My Flower family
My Kopelman family
And my daughters

Thank you
You taught me everything I know

Contents

Preface

I wrote this book without assuming anyone would ever read it. And yet I wrote for you, the person reading this right now.

If it feels personal for you, then I am so happy, because it was personal for me. I didn't write it in any particular format. This is not a sweeping life story but an elaboration on times in my life as I remembered them. I asked myself from time to time, over the course of exactly one year, "What should I revisit?" or "What stories should I tell?" Because to me, these are stories. My publisher wanted to call this a memoir at first, but that didn't sound right. "Memoir" seemed heavy to me, and I want this to be light.

This is a book you can dip into and read when you want. A book to read when you want. But I can only hope that every once in a while it catches you inconveniently feeling something. It was inconvenient writing it with two young daughters. They are my universe, and I felt terrible pulling myself away from them to write. Ever. But every mother knows how this feels.

However, I discovered over this year that being a mother is at times hardest in the transitions. Pulling yourself away you feel like the devil. But once you do, you can be more present. And the gift is that once you pull away from your responsibilities, you can fully be a parent. It's being present that matters most. And when I was writing and I shut my door, I would let the inspiration flow. For some reason I had to write this book. I have become more private every year, and yet these stories were beating at the door of my heart, screaming, "Let me out!!!!!!!!!!!!!!" Maybe it was that I have always dreamed of being a writer. Those people who do the typing and the transporting are my heroes. I have never been able to do that. I have never been brave enough. Smart enough. Had enough to say. I had not exercised those abilities in my life. And now I have, alone in a room, and yet as I say in the book, you do nothing in this life alone. And most of all, you do not live alone. And therefore we all have stories to tell.

These are mine.

Wildflower

Out there in the world of chaos
All the concrete and fumes
People with determination behind the wheel
The soles of their feet wiser
Some faces with souls of routine
Others with high hope of their destination
Among all the human and industrial invention
My eyes find a tiny wildflower
With pretty yellow petals
And a brown button nose
Reminding me that there is beauty everywhere
A compass of nature
A second of stillness in my mind
As my heart races to the rhythms
Of it swaying in the wind
You are that Flower,
Reminding me of what is real

West Hollywood, 1978

BIRDS OF PARADISE

In 1975, the neighborhood I grew up in, West Hollywood, was a colorful place. It had the aesthetic of old cars, the way everyone idealizes Havana, and the wildly different styles of architecture from one house or apartment building to another. Santa Monica Boulevard with its pimps and old movie theaters. And the drag queens, that was just a fact that the kids from our hood grew up with: "Mom, is it a man or a woman?" and then the parents could probably individually decide how to answer. But having this colorful world all around is what made this area so interesting.

My mother, then named Ildiko Jaid, raised me as a single mother there. She was an aspiring actress who did bit parts here and there, and worked two jobs at the infamous Comedy Store and also at the notorious music venue the Troubadour. She was living a life around many wild artists and the whole scene of that era was very hedonistic. She was also friends with many gay men, and so that just became a part of life too. Their style and their wit were comforting. We lived on Poinsettia Place in a tiny duplex that had a giant wall of bougainvillea up the front, about twenty-five feet high, which to a little kid seems like a skyscraper, and it made our place stand out on the street. This dramatic, hearty flower with its deep maroon made me so happy. I was so in love with its color, and it taught me that beauty could live in a seedy area. Not only live but also be strong!

We lived on one side of the duplex, and our neighbor on the other side was Joanie Goodfellow. Her son was Daniel Faircloth, and it was only after, years later, that it struck me how distinct their names were. At the time she was just another single mom, much like mine, whose man had taken off, leaving just her and the kid. I still can't remember the name of the father, but I remember he was from somewhere like Delaware or Denver—neither place I knew, or geography in general—but every time she talked about him I would picture him in a western shirt or cowboy boots, don't ask me why. Men left and moms worked were the messages I was receiving from our lives in this duplex.

I still have no clue what Joanie did. Joanie was eccentric. She had electric-blue or neon-green hair, and would slink around the apartment like an exhibitionist with very little clothing, often having two cockatoos perched one on each shoulder. At first I was wide-eyed about it, but eventually I would have been more shocked to find it any different. Strange what we get used to.

Her son, Daniel, became my best friend, even though I didn't even know what that was at the time. But we would sell apples up and down the street and beat the shit out of each other. A typical West Hollywood friendship, I think. When it was time for him to go to bed, every night was the same routine. Joanie would say, "OK, time for bed," and he would immediately start climbing the curtains in their living room. It was as if he was in a gym, making his way up the rope. He would scream, "I don't waaaaannnnnaaaaa go to beeeeeddddddddd." When he had almost reached the top, Joanie would just pluck him off and throw him in the bedroom down the hall. Our duplexes each had two bedrooms. It seemed spacious to me. I was actually proud that these single moms could provide a two-bedroom situation for us kids. To all have our own rooms was nothing to scoff at.

There was also a teeny-tiny backyard with a cheap swing set and an avocado tree. To say that I ate ten avocados a day off that tree was no exaggeration. I loved that tree. It nourished me, and other than the cascading bougainvillea out front, it was my only source of nature. Just like me, the tree and the flower bush didn't mind that they were existing among crime and X-rated movie theaters. We were all just really happy in our fantasyland. In fact the significance of the avocado tree is still as strong as can be for me. I even have it in my will that I want to be buried under one, or have some of my ashes put there. Some avocado tree preferably on a hill that is nowhere near anything this time. Just up on a hill on a rolling mountain, preferably with an ocean view. I can dream!

For now, my nature consisted of the things living and growing at Poinsettia Place, and most jarring to me was the strange-looking plant on the side of the house. There was a narrow, long driveway that led from front to back, all concrete. It was where my mom would park her beat-up, discolored temperamental old Volkswagen Karmann Ghia. But alongside the driveway, lining the house, were plants called birds-of-paradise. They have a long, pale green stalk, with bright orange pointy petals and some blue accents. Picture the colors that the gas stove burner emits. Blues and oranges. They are spiky and look like they belong in Palm Springs or the Galápagos. Not hidden in West Hollywood. I would stare at these things, wondering if they were plants or flowers. They looked like angry flamingos. They scared me. I would look for the eyes, but I was always afraid they could come to life and bite me. I stayed away, but then would tiptoe around them every once in a while with sick fascination. In a life where, as a kid, I had many questions about what was this or what was that, this vegetation was the embodiment of everything in the neighborhood: It couldn't be defined.

Joanie and Daniel moved out when I was around four or five. I was sad. But then this really nice couple with a Dalmatian named McBarker moved in. Gina and Joel were a cute, attractive, lovely couple, and I took right to them. Especially Joel, as I was starved for anything "straightforward," like an unconfusing male! There was no "are you gay, straight, a man or woman?"—I know you're not my dad, but as Mr. Rogers would say, won't you be my neighbor! I loved them. We all celebrated Christmas together on their side of the duplex. Joel came out in Christmas-patterned pants, and Gina was just a beautiful Latina woman who was in small movie parts and Budweiser calendars. Joel was an actor too. We all opened presents, and I was just having the most normal Christmas Day and soaking up every second of this traditional moment in our lives. Joel gave me a teddy bear. I named it Bailey Bear, after Joel's last name, and I just couldn't have loved it more. They were a great couple. When they got married, we got to go to their wedding, and even when they had the rare fight and I could hear it on our side of the thin duplex walls, it was comforting to me to hear a man's voice. They made me feel so safe. They were good people, and they were straightforward in a town that was full of cryptic lives.

These were happy years, the most stable years I'd ever had. We lived in this house for seven years, all the time I could remember. But when I turned seven, after *E.T.* had premiered and I was starting to get a lot of other film offers, my mother's and my life were changing. I will never forget one night when we were all waiting to go to dinner together at the duplex, and my mom pulled in with a brand-new BMW 320i. I couldn't understand. Where was the beat-up Karmann Ghia? What was happening? Change felt scary. We all went to eat, and I felt like I was on a bad trip. I didn't like it. A few weeks later, I came home and looked up in horror as I walked up to the duplex. Someone had cut down the bougainvillea bush. I started to cry. This was the entire cover for our house. It was beauty. It was nature. It was the thing that made me say, we don't really have money, but you don't need money to marvel at something! This giant waterfall of burgundy was just gone. I ran back to the avocado tree, terrified. It was still there, but it was completely shaven. That was the day I learned the word "pruned." My heart sank. It was just a trunk and branches. I was told it would grow back and this is what had to be done in order for it to be healthy. I was sick. We had lived here for seven years and no one had pruned or manicured anything and everything was fine! Was there a new gardener? The car? I ran around in circles. I felt like everything was crashing down around me.

And then it dawned on me: The birds-of-paradise, what state were they in? I made my way slowly over to the side of the house where Joel now parked his old Mustang. Were those freaky birds-of-paradise unscathed, or had they got the royal treatment too? I made my way around the corner, one foot in front of the other, waiting for the reveal . . . and then I saw them. Green stalks with no heads. They had not escaped whoever came here and took it all away. They were no longer intimidating. They had been guillotined, and there they stood, awaiting rebirth. And for the first time, I felt heartbreak. They didn't deserve it. Sure, they were different. Sure, I had never really understood them. But right now

I just wanted to hold them and tell them it would be OK. And then I realized I didn't know if it would. I didn't understand any of this.

Later, my mom came home; she had quit her job, and told me that she was going to manage my career full-time. And then she dropped the big bomb: "We're moving to the valley! I bought a house, and we are going to have a real home!"—as if it was some selling point. I was disgusted. Great. I will be the breadwinner. We will leave Joel and Gina and McBarker and go move to what felt like a planet away. As if I had been lobotomized, we packed our things and moved into our new home, indeed in Sherman Oaks, in 1983. It's why I still talk like a valley girl. That cadence snuck into my life at that spongelike age of eight and never left. I will be talking to a high-powered CEO and I will hear myself in my own head and think, friggin Sherman Oaks!

The only good news was that the house had a pool. But I missed Poinsettia Place. I never heard from the team of Goodfellow and Faircloth, but I always wish them well. Years later, when I was taking care of my dad when he had cancer, I wondered if Daniel was reconnecting with his father somewhere out in the world. I wondered if Joanie still dyed her hair. I wondered how Joel and Gina were. I heard they had kids and possibly moved to the valley as well. I think about that avocado tree.

As an adult, I was determined to get back to headquarters, and I moved back to West Hollywood. I was in charge of my destiny now and I bought a house right in the old neighborhood. I wanted to be in the familiar.

Things have cleaned up a bit, and the city has spruced up the joint. I take my kids to the same park I went to as a kid, and today I took my daughter Olive for a lollipop in the old convenience mart I would go to with Daniel to buy goodies with the change we made from selling our apples.

Currently, I work with a landscape architect named Marcello. Marcello and I have long discussions about plantings and, most important, prunings. He knows that we cannot cut as much as a leaf without deep discussion and reasoning. He sees me start to flip, but I am incredibly respectful. He is the expert, so he takes me through why he has to cut the leaves off the vines every year. He tells me that they literally get a fungus that will kill them unless we trim them annually. He helps me understand that it's death or trimming, and these are my options.

He is delicate with me, and I try humor with him. I jokingly tell him that I will cut off his limbs and chase him around with them. He laughs. Yet there is a small part of him that thinks I am a little crazy. Maybe there is 1 percent of him that doesn't think I am joking. Maybe that's good. We also have those days where he can see that look in my eye, and we go and buy bougainvillea by the truckload and do large plantings. I plant as much bougainvillea as possible around my house, and I find new areas to put more and more all the time. He and I are cultivators together.

When my grandfather John Barrymore would hang out with W. C. Fields, W. C. apparently was obsessed with his rose garden. Behind his desk he had a large chalkboard and written on it one day, in large letters, was "Bloom you bastards! Bloom!" A man after my own heart. I love flowers. I protect flowers. If I see a commercial for a spray that kills dandelions, I'm like "Why?" and it pains me. I am on the first line of defense of flowers.

And I wonder to this day if those birds-of-paradise ever grew their heads back. The ghosts of them bloom fresh in my memory all the time. They, like all of us in this neighborhood, were wild. Let us all be like them and defy tradition, and yet create our own traditions at the same time. Let us all be wildflowers!

Skydiving, 2000

FLYING HIGH

We had heard about a skydiving place not far from where we lived. Cameron Diaz and I were in a crazy mode where all we wanted to do was adventurous stuff. High off the rush of *Charlie's Angels* and training in kung fu for four months straight and then performing stunts for the next six, we had become total adrenaline junkies. We had just come back from a trip to the Tahitian Islands, where we scuba dived with sharks! It was amazing. Six-foot-plus grays and nurses swimming all around in a giant fishbowl of what would normally seem terrifying but was actually a peaceful descent to silence and awe sixty feet under water. I liked that you had to use signals and stop talking for a while and yet everyone could fully communicate.

At one point, when our guide took out a huge plastic bag of something that looked like mangled guts, my eyes bugged out, but then he took out a twelve-inch blade and sliced it open. The blood went everywhere and so came the sharks. I quickly motioned to him with a hand sweeping back and forth across my neck as if to say, "Enough! We're good, please don't chum the water anymore." It was crazy to be in a place where in the blink of an eye things could have gone very bad.

And yet we survived and loved every minute of it. So when we found out that there was a skydiving school about an hour away from Los Angeles, we immediately signed ourselves up and drove out to Perris, California, a total desert landscape.

When we arrived at the school we were met by a bunch of dudes. Hot doggers and bird chasers. I knew from first glance they were all up on my girlfriend's tip. And as long as no one was inappropriate, I just rolled with it. I am forever protective and chivalrous of my friend. She calls me her little man because in the first *Charlie's*, we dressed in disguise as men to break into Redstar tech facilities. I looked oddly like a very short James Spader, and she like a normal-height pencil-pushing CPA. And although I come up to her elbow, the name "little man" stuck.

Poo Poo (our mutual nickname for each other) and I have known each other since I was fourteen and she was sixteen. We met in West Hollywood back in the late '80s. There were two beautiful girls, both models, Cameron and Cory. Everyone ogled them, but most important they were both extremely nice and the opposite of cold. But they were cool.

We hung around in similar circles for many years. I liked any girl's girl and Cameron was definitely that. But it was when I called her, because I was producing *Charlie's Angels*, and dared her to come play that we became so close. She was shooting *Being John Malkovich*, and I arranged a phone call for us so that I could pitch her the movie because a script hadn't even been written. I talked about tone and what I wanted it to be, but I really stressed the sisterhood and the capability of these women to her. I said, "Girls want to do what boys do without losing the idea that they want love at the end of the day! They also love each other as women and they are stronger together. They want to kick ass and have fun." I knew she would get the spirit of women who supported each other and liked to laugh. That's who she has always been, and I knew we would have a blast! And we did. Well after the films ended, we continued our journey as friends and thrill seekers.

So here we were, two girls who wanted to jump out of a plane, and we were watching our instructional videos, which were terrifying, but worse, they make you sign your life away. Literally. You have to sign an "if I don't make it" contract. They tell you it's standard protocol. They also tell you that it's likely you will get cotton mouth on the plane ride up and to bring some water. What the hell was I doing? Just as I started to question if we had gone too far this time, they gave us our suits to change into. I noticed that hers was bright red and mine was canary yellow. We took our balled-up material and went into the changing rooms. The guys were kind of making jokes and yukking it up as we changed. I was starting to get the sense that these yahoos were holding themselves back from falling all over themselves for her. It was obvious that they were all salivating, and who wouldn't.

I was used to this. And as protective as I was, I got it completely. I loved her too! But in this cacophony of douchebaggery, I was more worried about the question "Are these the guys we want to possibly die with?"

I zipped up my suit, and we both emerged from our curtained makeshift dressing rooms at the same time. My eyes bulged. They had put me in a bright yellow rayon jumpsuit with a giant toucan across the entire front of it. I looked like an Oompa Loompa. Being on autopilot and contemplating my mortality while getting dressed, I was so distracted that I hadn't noticed that some jackass had chosen a full-on fucking clown suit for me. Not only did I feel worried, I also looked like a total idiot.

Then my eyes looked over, and they had given Cameron a skintight, painted-on red spandex onesie that literally let you make out every inch of her body. I wanted to punch these assholes. And there we were, Suzy Chapstick and Toucan Sam. They told us how good we looked, and I rolled my eyes and uttered "Fuck you" under my breath. They told us it was time to go, and the Froot Loops outfit went right out of my mind as the sound of the propellers kicking up outside the building took my full attention now.

We walked to the plane. We all had our packs and chutes on now, including an altimeter on my chest. I looked like a human dashboard, and we entered the open plane. It took off, and now I looked down at my altimeter and it said a thousand feet, and I looked out the window. It seemed really high. I turned to the instructor designated to me and yelled over the whirling air in the plane, "How many feet up do we go before we jump?" He looked at me with a shit-eating grin and said, "Ten thousand feet." Oh my GOD. OK. It looked good enough to me at two thousand feet, which we were now at, as we had gone up another thousand since I had last checked my chest meter one minute earlier. Wow. My tongue started to expand. I couldn't breathe, but most noteworthy was the infamous cotton mouth they spoke of. My tongue was a combination of sandpaper and felt. Water would not even begin to help the arid nature of my mouth as it would be like spitting on a forest fire.

At around eight thousand feet I just sat with my mouth open. It was a hollow sand trap and no longer resembled my mouth. My instructor turned to me and asked another in a series of stupid trivial questions. "So, what was E.T. like?" I simply couldn't answer. Words were not an option at this point, as my tongue had become a fat cashmere taquito. And before I knew it, everyone was starting to stand up and prepare for jumping out. I finally looked at Poo Poo. Having just scuba dived with her, I felt like we could communicate with our eyes. After a deep breath and a stare-down, I think we both telepathically said, "These guys are tools. But we came all this way, and it would be a shame to turn back now. They can get us where we need to go. And we need to go out of this plane and rock this goddamn dive!" Yes!

I felt better. Cowabunga. Let's do this. Just then, one of the guys said, "Who wants to go first?" Feeling my newfound bravado, I raised my hand. Again, I couldn't speak, so I figured my arm would tell everyone I was ready to go! We braced ourselves at the opening of the plane. We were to rock back and forth, tethered to our guides, just like we practiced down at the base training facility. We crouched down. My arms were wrapped across my chest like a mummy. They counted out loud. One. My tongue was at a new level of useless. Two. Oh my God, I'm really doing this. Three. OK, fuck it, let's dance.

And with that thought I threw myself out of the plane. Down, down, down we went. And it went on forever. The air was so forceful I couldn't breathe. I wondered how long this would go on because if I didn't die from the jump, I would definitely die from wind inhalation or lack of oxygen. In my periphery I saw Poo Poo going straight down headfirst, which actually makes you go faster, so even though she jumped out second, she was now passing me like a human bullet. I continued to hold my breath and prayed to get to the deployed chute part. Open open open!!!!!! Please, God, open!

And with that, after a one-minute-long free fall, my chute jerked me up in the air and canopied all around me. As it cascaded out and I started to glide through the air, aaaaaahhhhhh. This was the vision I had. This was the silence I craved. And I gently floated through the air like a soaring bird. I was overwhelmed by the peace I felt. I had made it. I was flying. And just like that, the guy I was tethered to started up on the dumb questions again. "So, you gonna make another movie soon?" Oh, Christ. Shut up!

I politely asked how long the gliding down would take and he said, "Oh, about ten minutes." "Great," I said, but what I meant was "Great, I have to listen to your shit for ten more minutes when all I want is to enjoy the landscape!" Unlike him, I knew I would not be doing this again anytime soon.

After what felt like an eternity, I landed smoothly, I'm happy to say. My instructor took my face and gave me a big grandmother kiss. Yuck. Thanks a lot. First you put me in this clown suit and now you try to grope me? Get me out of here. We got out of there as fast as possible, happy to have our lives and bodies intact. And we drove to the closest place we could find to get something to drink. There was a fast-food joint on the side of the road and we ran inside. Two sodas and two burritos later, we recounted our experiences in words—A, because we could now talk without being listened to, and B, because my mouth was functioning again.

Just as we got going and were quietly screaming about what we were each going through, Poo Poo bit into glass in her burrito. Well, if it's not one thing, it's another. You survive jumping out of a plane, but you almost die eating after. We just started laughing the hardest laugh you could imagine. We took off and drove back to Hollywood with the wind in our faces from the open windows of the car—although I think it's safe to say that I will never again experience wind in my face like that of a free fall at ten thousand feet.

Now we are older and she is still one of my closest friends. I was her bridesmaid, and she is my daughter Frankie's godmother. We still go on adventures all the time, but they are much more mellow. But that's the thing I love about my friend. She is always game. And I will always be her little man.

John Drew Barrymore

JOSHUA TREE

My dad. I don't really know where to begin other than to say he simply wasn't a "dad." He was this mythical creature. Part unicorn, part violent storm. And although he separated from my mom when she was pregnant, I somehow knew to forgive him. It's as if I could grasp as a kid that this horse was so wild, he couldn't be pinned down, and even if he could I am not sure you would want him around. This was the kind of man you saw in small doses. They were memorable. Sometimes dark, sometimes humorous, sometimes quotable. Example: When I was with him as a teenager he told me he needed food, and I asked him, "Oh yeah, are you hungry?" He looked at me wide-eyed and indignant. "Hungry? I was hungry since the day I was born!"

It made sense, I guess. Another time he was staying with me for a brief alternate-universe visit, and I needed security at my house for a short period. He came walking up my driveway and said, "Daughter, why do you need security? You've got me! I've got my nightstick and my third eye!" . . . Right.

No one would have ever guessed my father would have ended up being the man he was at that time. He was my grandfather John Barrymore's only son, and had been a promising actor when he was young. He had been gorgeous and dynamic, but he threw his career away in a total self-sabotage. Today he looked like a frail, homeless old hippie. More someone you would be trying to keep out than allow in. The truth is I never lived with my father. I never even had a dinner with both of my parents. I never knew the whole story of how my parents met and got together. They most likely met at the Comedy Store or the Troubadour. They had a tumultuous few years together and then separated before I was born.

My mother and father were both incapable of being parents, and I don't fault them for it. My therapist would disagree, but the truth is they gave me a great blueprint through their behavior of what not to do with my own kids. For starters, I will have so many thousands of dinners with my kids. They will sleep together and go to school and have a bedtime, and life will be so stable and consistent that they will complain until they grow up and realize that this is the better way! A stable, loving family is something that should absolutely, fundamentally never ever be taken for granted! I am lucky that I got dealt some cards that showed me what it's like to not have family, and I am much luckier to now have the chance to create my own deck! I will fight like William "Braveheart" what's-his-name to keep them protected and intact! I am a warrior. I am a soldier. I am a not-to-be-messed-with lion! I am a mother!

When I think about my dad, I think most about when he got cancer and I actually got to take care of him for a while. I was in my late twenties at the time. He got kicked out of the first hospice house I had put him in for disorderly conduct (weed and erratic behavior, which usually don't go together, but what can I say). I wasn't even surprised in the slightest, but I needed to find him somewhere to live because he needed medical attention 24-7 at this stage in his multiple myeloma, so hanging at my house was not an option. I finally found a place that would take him, and it actually had an ocean view, and we got him a long, thin pillow to block the scent of his weed from drafting underneath the door, and these people were saints at handling his unreasonable demands. No one could wear perfume around him: "Murderers, man!!" If someone had used detergent—"Oh man, you're killing me!"—he would order everyone to wash in nothing but Dr. Bronner's soap from head to toe ("You can even brush your teeth with it!" he said), and then he would douse himself in real lemon juice and olive oil. He was like a human salad. There were lemons everywhere. I'm talking hundreds. But those were his bottom lines. My father acted like Cleopatra on the throne of his temporary bed. Everything in his life was temporary. For as long as I knew him, or barely knew him, he was always coming from somewhere and going somewhere else. My father never had an apartment. No address to send a letter. No phone to call him if the mood struck. He didn't wear shoes! Even this crazy man's feet had to be free! He would roam Topanga Canyon in the '70s and '80s and just show up at my mom's duplex with David Carradine (of *Kung Fu*) and talk some crazy nonsense, usually wreak havoc on the joint, and then take off again. He and my mom would yell a battle of words and duel about who was wittier or who had made the last genius comeback. They fought like pathetic poets, but really my mom had just made a terrible choice in my dad and he wanted to be worshipped from afar without the dare of an expectation! I would just sit in the other side of the room and count the minutes until he would disappear again.

Then he would show up again at a random Christmas dinner at a friend's house, where my mom had taken me so that we might be somewhere more traditional and full of life as opposed to the Charlie Brown Christmas tree and single-momness of our home. We would be having dinner, and then I would hear sounds of chaos and commotion coming from the other room. He would then storm in and start ranting, and eventually would have to be escorted out by the hosts. He would do the same thing at a random Chinese restaurant—I don't even know how he found us. He would come crashing in like the Kool-Aid guy, and then a bunch of people would rally and literally take him outside. Yep. I was never really showing off to anyone, pointing, "That's my dad!!" I more just watched in awe.

Many years later, I hadn't seen him for about seven or eight years, and I stood next to him and he was around fiftysomething and the drugs and the road had taken his swagger away some and he just didn't seem like a threat in the slightest. So I went from damaged kid to "I could kick his ass" status, and the playing field just leveled and we could become friends. One time I told him I was mad at my mom, and he said, "Oh baby, you gotta kick the bag," as if to say I should let go of any resentment. "Um, OK." He was just this guy who literally didn't want to carry anything. Literally or metaphorically. And once again I left thinking, I'll see you when I see you. No pain. No attachments. No drama.

I would occasionally get some kind of carrier-pigeon-type communication from him, as this was all way before cell phones, and we would meet up in Joshua Tree. I would stay in some weird place he had for the weekend, bring my dogs, and we would go in some golf cart (again, where in the world did he get this golf cart?) and tool around in Joshua Tree National Monument. Just the two of us and Flossy and Templeton, my cool-customer, go-anywhere dogs, and I would just love these times. They were easy. Strange. Temporary. And usually gave me plenty of one-liners to laugh all the way home about.

He would talk about the flickering Buddha, quote Walt Whitman, but I really loved when he would share an anecdote about our family, the Barrymores.

He made it seem so real. All the Barrymores had passed away

before I was born, so there was no dynasty-like upbringing. But I could see why people thought I might have grown up that way. My grandfather was the great actor John Barrymore. They called him and my great-aunt Ethel and my great-uncle Lionel the royal family! I never knew any of them, and I wanted to more than words can ever describe. I would think about my grandfather all the time. Lots of my friends knew their grandparents so well, and I wished I could have that same luxury. I was particularly fascinated with my grandfather John. When my dad would talk about his own father, I would listen as if I was being let into this fairytale world, where dangers lurk but fantastical magical things can occur. He would talk about the legend of when my grandfather's body was stolen from the morgue by his friends, including W. C. Fields, Errol Flynn, a crazy poet named Sadakichi Hartmann, a painter named John Decker, and a writer named Gene Fowler (who wrote a famous book about my grandfather called *Good Night, Sweet Prince*).

So the legend goes, they stole his body, and in an attempt to give him one last party, they propped John up at a poker table with sunglasses on and a cocktail in hand and invited people over and had one last hell of a soiree. Well, you have got to hand it to them for not letting death be spoiled by such depressing sadness. They took a whole other approach. It's not one I recommend, per se, but this was the line of great loonies from which I come. They were talented, damaged, and I can't help but idealize them because it's all I have. And just like my grandfather's friends, I don't want to be sad about loss.

As my father was winding down and his days were numbered, I spent even more time at the hospice house. During the days I would walk around to stretch my legs and watch the other patients. There was an old couple I would stare at every day I was there. A woman, who was clearly the patient, would sit in a La-Z-Boy chair in the first-floor communal room where visitors could congregate. Her husband would sit with her, and sometimes he would just take her face with both hands and bring her face into his and they would just stay face-to-face for long periods of time. He would give her these old gummy kisses all over her face, and she would accept his affection, just sitting there with no strength to move. I don't know if he was making up for not doing it enough or if this was their routine, but all their years together had led to more love. More affection. More appreciation. A oneness that you would marvel at as I did. My father was upstairs with his weed and his lemons, but he was alone. Maybe he wanted it that way. He certainly alienated everyone along the way. But I would want to be the couple who kissed for hours. I went back upstairs.

Later that afternoon, I was sitting in a chair with a little dress on and no shoes, and my father was in bed, just quiet, which was very novel. He was thinking. I don't know when he had time to reflect, as he was always spouting out demands. Maybe he thought his thoughts in Joshua Tree. Maybe in the middle of the night. Maybe all those years in Topanga Canyon? But now, in this moment, he was gentle. I didn't know where his gaze was, and I wasn't totally sure what to do in the silence. But I sat there, patiently waiting to hear the next wild thing fly out of his mouth. "You were made perfect," he said, looking at my feet. He looked up into my face and deep into my eyes. "You were made perfect."

For the first time in my life I didn't know what to say. So I just took in the moment. And told myself to remember this forever. For it was his way of taking my face and telling me he loved me.

He died a few months later. And when I picked up his stuff, there was only Dr. Bronner's soap bottles and lemon rinds and his old floppy, threadbare bandanas. So I kept a purple one and threw the hippie detritus away. And we planned a ceremony where we would let his ashes fly all over his "home away from no home" ... Joshua Tree.

I drove out there late at night and got a room in the middle of the desert, and the hotel had forgot to leave a key, so I slept in my car. When the sun just started coming up and it wasn't so terrifyingly dark, I looked for a key, and I found one taped in a strange place with a note for me, but I would have needed my third eye and a flashlight to find it, as my dad would have said. I walked through the dirt to my little room and lay down for a while. And just as I was falling asleep, my door slowly swung open on its own.

And a ray of sun came pouring in. "Dad?" I said out loud as I felt a field of energy pass through the room. I sat up in bed for a while, silent, until it felt like I could get up and respectfully shut the door. I got back in bed. Was it him? It could have been him. Why not? There are no rules.

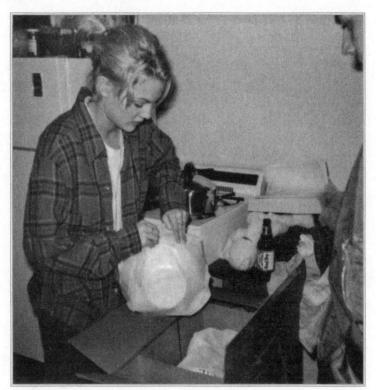

First apartment, at age fourteen

MY BEAUTIFUL LAUNDRETTE

When I was fourteen, I was emancipated by the courts. It's no secret that I had to part ways from my mother because we had driven our relationship into the ground. She had lost credibility as a mother by taking me to Studio 54 (so wrong but so fun) instead of school. And I was out of control due to working since I was eleven months old and what that had done to my childhood, which made me grow up too fast. Work was a very positive thing in my life, and sadly it had been taken away because my mother also put me in an institution because she felt helpless. But when people found out, they just wrote me off as damaged goods, and I sadly understood that. I was never unprofessional, but I was on a hiatus from being employable. And when I turned fourteen and wanted to start my life over, I wanted to do things on my own terms.

On the day of my hearing, my mother was there in full support of my emancipation, which would mean me living on my own. I felt so sad, but too much had happened. The judge walked in and the day went on in a blur. People testified, but it wasn't heavy or dark. It was a way to ask, Should this kid become an adult? At the end of the day the judge looked at me and said these words, which stuck with me: "I can turn the clock forward, but I can never turn it back. Are you ready for that?" "Yes," I said. "OK," he said with a slight smile, "I hereby pronounce you an adult! Legally." My mom and I hugged, knowing things would be different, but things were always just too different, and that was why this needed to happen.

I walked out an eighteen-year-old in the eyes of the state of California. This was gonna be fun.

First on my checklist, I needed . . .

1. Apartment!

I looked all over West Hollywood, my favorite neighborhood and where I had grown up. I found a place in the back of a building my friend Justine was living at. Great! Although it was off an alleyway in a notoriously "don't walk around here at night" neighborhood, I was happy that my girlfriend was a stone's throw away. She lived there with her boyfriend, and I particularly loved when they fought. I was always secretly willing them to break up because I would fantasize about Justine and me getting our own bungalow somewhere! Whenever she and Darren had a blowout, she would come hang out in my place, and then Darren would perform some big mea culpa outside. He would grab the bars on the window (did I mention the apartment had to have bars covering every window?), but to Darren they were like a stage prop. Stanley Kowalski, the '90s former-model version, would hang from these bars and scream how "he needed her!" And how it was "her fault too." Blah blah blah. She always let him back in. Whatever. Boys were a whole other chapter that I knew I wasn't up for yet . . . what's next?

Oh right.

2. Job.

Justine worked at a coffeehouse in the valley, but she had a car and I was two years away from getting my driver's license, so I was going to have to act global and think local. Inspired by Justine, I looked at the coffeehouse near us, the Living Room, which happened to be one of the big LA hot spots at night. It was the start of the 1990s, and coffeehouses were where everyone hung out. People poured out onto the street every night, as if it was a big art opening, but it would just be a random Tuesday.

I wasn't great at my job. I wasn't really great at anything. I had only done two things: acted and had wild life experiences. But neither of those prepares you for the real world. At all! My apartment when I came back to it was a mess. It smelled like wood from the IKEA pieces I had bought that still lay in the boxes (how in the world were those EVER going to get erected?), and my fridge was literally a science project. I only had takeout cartons and to-go boxes that had lost their shapes, but much worse . . . they had all grown spores. Yes, it's true. I didn't even know you were supposed to throw them away. Somehow my nutty fourteen-year-old brain would put the half-eaten food back in the fridge rather than in the garbage. Even if I knew, somewhere in my juvenile brain, that I probably wasn't ever going to return to that General Tso's chicken, I would just place it next to a half-eaten sandwich. It was as if they should just live together. Like an edible *Toy Story* where the fridge comes to life when I shut the door.

But somehow looking every night at the growing laundry pile was the thing that really sent me over the edge. I stared at the massive pile of clothes. It soon became a bubbling blob-like horror movie that would start to have the *Jaws* theme every time I looked at it. The chords of the piano were slow, *duh na, duh na, duh na duhna duhna*, and then at the height of the music, where you know that gosh-darn shark is coming, I would quickly look away and shut my eyes and the music would end. *Ahhhhhhh*. The hum of my old fridge and the moaning sounds of the alley cats would soothe me. Sleep. But sleep was scary too. Somewhere in West Hollywood I was very alone. I needed something to comfort me. Something to fall in love with. Something romantic. Something transportive. Something safe. I opened a classic novel I had acquired and read myself to sleep. Somewhere around when the sun came up, I felt safe enough to close my eyes, my book right next to me like a stuffed animal or the lover I wasn't old enough to have.

I went to work the next day, and I could tell my boss, who had hired me on the novel idea of having a washed-up former child actor behind the counter, was patient with all my learning curves but was also irritated with me. "You must be there for the muffin deliveries! At seven a.m. sharp! Or else we won't have anything to put in the damn cases!!!" "OK, got it." It was a little in-one-ear-out-the-other. Another time he came in when I was doing dishes (which, come to think of it, probably subconsciously made me realize you actually had to "do" dishes rather than just put everything in the sink and pray, like I did at home), but he walked in and said, very sharply and exasperatedly, "Don't use the abrasive side of the brush!!!! All the pastry cases are getting scratched and foggy and you can't see what's inside!!!!!" "Oh, you're right! I thought it was getting it cleaner, but yeah, I see what you mean! Huh, I was wondering why that was happening." He looked at me with wide eyes and clearly went in the other room to mutter "idiot" under his breath. But again, he liked me and I had truly ruined some stuff. He had every right to be miffed.

I went back to my apartment after work, feeling like a bit of a loser. I looked around the dirty apartment. Everything I touched turned to shit. The fridge! The sink! The furniture that lay lifeless on the floor in fifty pieces. And the laundry! I didn't even know what I was wearing because everything I owned was in that basket, taunting me . . . AAAAAAAARRRRRRRGGGGGGGGGGGGGGGG. I hurled myself on the bed and clutched my pillow, staring at the wall all night. As the sun crept into the creepy alley outside my bedroom window, I knew I had survived another night. But this wasn't what I pictured when I left that courthouse with a skip in my step. Something had to give. I loved a self-improvement movie montage and I had to actually create one! Cue the music! OK, what did I need?

First, basics!

Toilet paper.

Sponge.

Soap.

Vacuum. (Intimidating!)

A man to put my furniture together.

Bedside table.

Lamp.

More books for that table.

Yeah, books, books were great! Books make me happy and help
me feel not so alone.

I chipped away at things one by one. But where the montage really started to soar was when I walked into a store to buy a laundry basket. There were all sorts of shapes and sizes, a whole wall of baskets. After holding different ones—as I knew I would be hoofing it several blocks to a Laundromat and I needed it to fit my body—I picked one and walked out with my brand-new vessel.

I bought detergent, bleach, and fabric softener. I grabbed my book and enough clothes to fill the basket sensibly and headed out the door. In my maiden voyage to the Laundromat, the whole way I was talking to myself... *Bleach first, detergent, wait, first cycle has bleach and detergent? That doesn't sound right. And the liquid fabric softener goes in the dryer? But isn't that going to make the clothes wet all over again?* I was very confused. *It doesn't seem like all three go into the wash? What? No!* I had given myself a stomachache. I walked in. I went to the machines. Which ones were which? Was this the washer or the dryer? What the hell? The circle shapes all around started to close in on me. I was Michael Keaton in *Mr. Mom* before he figures it all out! I was screwed. I just stood there. After a while, like a kid cheating on a test, I just started to spy on whatever other people were doing. *OK, that guy is pulling out wet clothes, so that must be the WASHER. Aha! Got it! Right.* It was also the kind of place where some of the washers were upright so the washer and the dryer looked the same, stacked on top of each other, which confused me so much because I was convinced all the water would come pouring out and I would make the biggest fool out of myself ever.

Eventually I had put some clothes in the washer, but then, *Do I put the liquid right in the clothes??? Wait, is this going to stain everything??? Oh God! And the bleach smells likes it's going to disintegrate my clothes on the spot!!!* Needless to say I put the bleach directly on the clothes and then I put the liquid fabric softener right in the dryer.

When I pulled out the Dalmatian-spotted jeans and the gummy towels, I knew I had done it all wrong, but there was always a next time and the next time would include Justine! I clearly needed a tutorial.

She came with me and gave me some tips and direction! It was a revelation! Of course! It all made such sense! Wow! The whole movie went from '80s comedy to glorious black-and-white! Yes, the opposite! But that's what I wanted in this new world I was creating for myself. It was the romance I was waiting for. Think old French movie!

Every weekend I would look forward to this ritual. I didn't feel alone there. I could be domestic, read my book, and eat some Chinese from the place next door in a carton with chopsticks. Everything fell into place, and I got so good at laundry that it became a point of pride. I loved stain removal. The art of getting your whites white. Pouring in my fabric softener and bleach so that I was more of a chef making a stew getting the ratios and flavors just right! And once I had finished my classic novel, I was excited to go to the bookstore and get a new one. I read books by Tolstoy, Jane Austen,

Joan Didion, Bukowski, John Fante, and Kurt Vonnegut. *The Fountainhead. To Kill a Mockingbird.* I read everything. What was my next adventure going to be?

As I roamed the book aisles, I had a realization that I had dropped out of school. Once I was emancipated, I just simply dropped out. Oh my God!!! I had a pit in my stomach again. What was I going to do? I had been on film sets my whole life, receiving three hours a day of tutoring. I hated when I went back to school because kids were merciless, a chapter you are supposed to face, but fuck it, I had enough to face at this point, I wasn't going back voluntarily, but what??? I didn't want to be uneducated. Oh my God, oh my God???? Just when I had mastered laundry, I was panicking all over again. What did I want to learn? What was my calling? Tears. *I don't know. I know acting, but that's gone for now, and I don't know if they will have me back.* People thought I was crazy—even though I wasn't, I just grew up too fast! Aaaarrrrrr-gggghhhhhhhhh. *OK, pull it together.* The walls of books started to envelop me. I looked at all the bindings and the jackets and shelves and the titles and the fonts and I started to come back to earth. The book jackets soothed me, a ritual I enjoy to this day. *Books? Book smart? I can read. I love books. Everyone seems to brag about being well-read. Books not only give me pleasure, they are good for me! Healthy. Screw it! I will create my own school! If I can live on my own, I can self-educate too! I will buy a dictionary and study every word. I will steep myself in all the things I love! I love laundry!*

I love books! I love music! I think I like art (go to museums, quick!).
I decided right then and there I would not be defeated. Failure was
not an option! I would create my own curriculum.

And so I did just that! I read! I cleaned! I worked! Oh God,
work! Back at the coffeehouse, my boss was having another "you
suck at this" moment with me. And as I was explaining another
thing I had messed up, he looked at me with those saucer eyes of
his one last time and said to me with clenched teeth . . . "Why
don't you go out and find yourself!" And even though he was half
trying to get rid of me, he was half right! I looked around: This
wasn't it. This wasn't my destiny.

I quit that day. Went back to my apartment, went right up to
Justine's door, and knocked with fervor (word of the day from my
annotated dictionary) until she opened it. "If I found us a new
place to live, would you ever want to move out and be roommates
and get the hell out of this shit hole?" She looked at me. "Well,
Darren and I just broke up, so sure! I'm in." Yaaaaaaaaaaay! A
roommate!!!! This might actually become fun! I ran back to my
place and started circling apartments for rent in the paper. Listening to the cats fighting in the alley, I looked out my window and
waited, as I did each morning, for the sun to come up to tell me
everything was going to be OK. And it was. I wasn't scared anymore. I was ready! And even though it was only laundry, it taught
me how to tackle everything moving forward. You fall in love and
try to conquer by way of mastering it!

My hero, Nan

TAURUS

When I woke up in the hospital, I glanced over and took a deep look at my new baby girl, who I had decided with my husband to name Frankie. She looked peaceful and sweet after her journey into the world—what a ride, huh, kid? I watched her, and after a little while she really looked at me. She had need in her eyes; my first daughter, Olive, was born independent and has never given me that needy look to this day. As much as I loved having this moment, something felt strange. I started feeling like a roller-coaster free fall was happening in my stomach. My head clenched tight, and tears started to pour out of me uncontrollably. Then came the sounds. Because I couldn't keep them inside. The wailing sobs were loud, and as I gasped for air it hit me . . . Frankie looked like my mom.

Like my mother, Frankie is also a Taurus in the astrological realm of life. And here she lay, looking at me, and I felt so many emotions that I simply could not classify them individually. This was a mosaic of things that made no sense together, yet if I broke it down, it might help me stop convulsing.

OK, number one, I asked myself, what is my worst fear? Well, the answer was easy; my biggest emotional button in life is my mother. I am a girl trying to be a woman, and being a mother first now, but I was being dragged and hog-tied back to childhood stuff that maybe I have never put to bed.

OK, I said to myself, you know that this is your biggest issue, but is it having a girl of your own and the fear of repeating any- thing that took place in your own childhood? I calmed myself by thinking through the last year and a half with Olive, my Libra, and how my life is as safe and consistent, stimulating and loving, as it could possibly be. There is proof of an existence that quells my worst fear!

OK, next. Is it that she looks like her? No, because she looks like me too, and yes, of course we both are going to resemble peo- ple in our families on both sides. But when Olive was born, she had the biggest, most beautiful wide-apart cat-shaped mega-eyes that there was already a point of difference. She actually seemed to take a bit after my mother-in-law, Coco, whom I cannot begin to describe how much I love, worship, and am simply in awe of. Coco is elegant, kind, smart, worldly, and a great, great, great mother! Her maiden name is Franco, and it was an inspiration for Frankie.

But Frankie was looking more like my family here in this hospital in Los Angeles, California, on April 22, 2014, and I was facing something I had managed to avoid with Olive. I was being asked if I could dig deep and heal this pain from the relationship I had with my Taurus mother while I was looking at my Taurus daughter.

I was born in 1975 to a single mother who was doing her best while still being young herself. She would actually never tell me her age—one of many strange mysteries I had with this woman—but I gather she was in her midtwenties when she had me. Still very much a hedonist, she brought me up with zero protection, zero consistency, and, as is known, we parted ways when I was fourteen, and we have rarely spoken since. I still support her—I must know that she is taken care of or I simply cannot function. I am grateful to this woman for bringing me into this world, and it would crush me to know she was in need anywhere. It is not who I am to harbor any anger for the fact that our life together was so incredibly unorthodox. I want only to say thank you to her, because I love my life and it takes every step to get to where you are, and if you are happy, then God bless the hard times it took you to get there. No life is without them, so what are yours, and what did you do with the lessons? That is the only way to live.

Another philosophy I have is that nothing is taken away without it being replaced, and with that truth enters the love of my life when I was nineteen years old in Seattle, Washington. I was at a bar with friends, I was making a movie up there, and it was the '90s, a very wild and inspired time for music and culture. But movies were the only thing on my mind. I had done a western film about two years before, and the whole experience made me want to make movies about girls. Capable girls. Girls who want to do what boys do but who still want to love the boys and want to run and tell their girlfriends about it and have each other's backs. I was figuring out who I wanted to be in the world, and I would sit around making mixtapes and trying to dream up what I could in life.

So there I was, sitting there in a booth, and my friend Jim said, by the way, my sister Nan is coming to meet us; she will be here for a few days. Great! And in walks this blond-haired, blue-eyed, big-teeth Breck girl with the most winning, warm, ingratiating smile I had ever seen. Nancy Juvonen was a girl who sang the songs of John Denver. She worked on planes as a flight attendant. She did semesters in Costa Rica and England. She worked on a dude ranch in Wyoming. She grew up in San Francisco and New Hampshire. Her life was about adventure and trying things. She was organized like no one I had ever met. She charted and diagramed everything and was a great planner and loved "board vision." You would hear her say things like "slow and steady wins the race," and she loved words like "EARN." She would become my partner in business. She would take me in like a sister; she would change my whole world in so many important ways. Nancy Juvonen is the replacement for the absence of family. She was my gift in life. And she is a Taurus.

Nan and I would start to actually articulate our vision when we started with our company, Flower Films. We wanted to tell stories. In the era of the early '90s power-suit woman, we vowed we would not abandon our JanSport backpacks. But what we would do was constant homework. We studied everything. We made lists on everything. We read everything. And we built relationships with people we admired and respected rather than party with the beautiful people.

We created a cozy, house-like environment at Flower Films on Sunset Boulevard. Nan's office was warm and truly lived in. That's where all our conversations and dreams took place. Her office was warm and utterly organized, and everything was labeled. Inbox, outbox, pictures hanging on the wall, pillows, and mantras by Abraham Lincoln in little frames placed on her desk. My office was a case study in disorganization, with papers all over my desk and no feng shui whatsoever. We did Christmas cards every year together, and it felt like we were creating traditions I just never had. In life outside the office we would road-trip across America in an RV. We would travel the world. We would adopt dogs. But the most important thing to know is that Nan never let me get away with anything..."YOU'RE LATE, and your time management sucks. You are selfish, and when you walk into a room apologizing for being late you are making it all about you. You are causing yourself and everyone else distractions and anxieties, and if you were just on time you could avoid all of this drama, for everyone." Jesus.

I was always hurt in the moment. One time I called her to tell her I wanted to direct. "You're not ready. You're too disorganized and you're still late and you cannot waste people's money and time. That is not leadership, and directors are leaders." I told her I would call her back and hung up and burst into tears.

"Don't ever drink and drive! Vote!" All of these wonderful things my parents should have taught me. I was so grateful for her tough love because it let me know time and again she cared, and for the record I was never late when I directed, thanks to her. She was willing to fight to help me get to my better self.

No matter what we go through, we always come out stronger. I have spent most holidays of my life with her family; she was the maid of honor at my wedding; and she is the family I never had until I made my own. And she still is. Twenty-two years she has been my beacon of light and goodness. She's also the most fun person ever. And if you're looking for the best advice on love, look no further. We've made many films about relationships, and on one particular one called *Fever Pitch*, she met her husband, Jimmy Fallon, and the perfect girl met the perfect guy. And although she hates when I call her perfect, to me she is.

Most of all, Nan was there to always teach me that if you stay emotionally balanced and responsible in life you are able to have the real joy. The earned joy. Back when we were just starting out, she lived in a small bachelorette apartment in West Hollywood. I remember walking in and seeing a yellow sign on her fridge that said "HAPPINESS IS A CHOICE." I stared at it. I loved it, but it took me twenty years to realize that it's the word "choice" that is so powerful. You must make that choice all the time. And the people I follow in life are the kind of people who are capable of making that choice all the time. Consistently.

She would also tell me that when I felt lost, the best thing to do was write! And as a lover of journals, this really spoke to me. And wouldn't you know it, another lady I love, Kate Capshaw Spielberg (Scorpio!) got me a five-year journal after Olive was born. And when I was a brand-new mother and experiencing fear and worry like I have never felt, this pink leather-bound journal was delivered to my door with a note that read, "Start writing to your daughter and keep it up every day! Love, Kate." I held this care package of a journal in my hand and I thought of what Nan always said. And I have written in it every day of my life since then, chronicling Frankie's and Olive's lives; and when my daughters are older, it will be my gift to them.

So who was I in this hospital room? Was I a damaged kid with mother issues, or was I a woman who has gone out there and fought hard for my lessons and actually found great role models? Great people, like Nan, have led me and lifted me out of feeling helpless or scared and given me power. Now I need to pass on this

49

wisdom and strength. Was I going to cower in this room when this kid, this new beautiful baby, needs me? Hell no. I got up, so sore and groggy, and picked up my baby Taurus. And I kissed her face over and over. I vowed, just as I did with Olive, that I would always be her warrior. I am their Pisces mother. Mother of dragons! I am strong. I have learned. I love Love and have plenty to give. It is my powerful destiny that I am supposed to raise two good girls into two great women! All right. Here we go, my beautiful little girls. Here we go.

Tokyo, 1982

THE SCHOOL OF *E.T.*

In 1982, in Culver City, California, I was auditioning for a film called *Poltergeist*. The producer was taking the auditions because the director was unavailable. His name was Steven Spielberg. And when I went into the room we started talking. I guess I did the same thing with him that I was starting to do with other people, which is lie. I was six, and I had basically developed a crazy alternate life in which I had skills like cooking and all kinds of brothers. I had zero siblings, and of course I didn't know how to make my way around a kitchen.

But the biggest thing in life that was currently taking up all my time was my so-called drumming. I was in an imaginary band called the Purple People Eaters, and my style was more punk rock than pop. In my room at Poinsettia Place I had posters all over my bedroom wall of Blondie and Superman, Kiss (which gave me nightmares, but I insisted on keeping it up), and of course Pippi

Longstocking. She was my ultimate hero. She could hold up a horse with her superhuman strength. She could show you how to have fun when you didn't exactly have family around. She could clean with brushes on her feet like ice skates, and she loved to travel. Every day in Pippi's world was a chance to go down the Nile or fight pirates. She made you feel like there was nothing you couldn't do if you put your mind to it.

Of course, I had told myself somewhere in my head that a healthy imagination is a good thing. And girls that rock are the way to go! So when I met Steven, I was in this state where the sky was the limit on what a girl could do, and he rewarded that with telling me I wasn't right for this movie. My heart sank.

But there was good news. He himself was directing a film called *A Boy's Life*, and would I come meet on that instead? Sure. I calculated in my head that I was too colorful for this project, but maybe his other one I was more suited for. I left the office and figured that if I got a callback for that film, I would know he was serious; if I never heard from him again, well, I would know he was just being nice, and I would try to capture the next job in my butterfly net with my skills and my stories.

My mom got a call a few weeks later from Marci Liroff, who was the woman working with Mike Fenton and Jane Feinberg, the casting directors for Steven's film. Well, I thought, this guy kept his word, how cool! And back in I went to meet with him. Now, I was thinking, I have already told him my usual rhetoric and wild tales, what am I going to wow him with now? And I started working up some bits on the way over.

I was very confident and precocious at that age. Now when I walk into a room, I survey it with humility and take in how I might best disarm people and yet bring them together. But that morning, when I was six, walking into a room with four adults, I had swagger. They all sat around observing me and asking questions. I was a dry-witted, lying, thieving six-year-old, and I just wanted to win the job and go on an adventure! Jobs cured the loneliness that I wouldn't have known how to classify but strongly felt. But here, right now, I had an audience! And I wanted to make the most of it. So after my made-up tales and small talk that was larger than life, I was mostly directing it to Steven because I knew that he was buying it; but once it was winding down, they all turned to each other and started talking as if I wasn't in the room. They do that in auditions. And you are expected to entertain yourself and look so distracted that you can't hear their hushed tones four feet away. I sat there, wondering when they would turn their attention back to me. I felt small. Scared all of a sudden.

What if they said thank you and that was it, which had happened plenty of times to me. I had been acting since I was eleven months old. My mother was working nights, but she thought I could make money during the day. It started with a Gainse-Burger puppy chow audition. According to her there were so many babies in the waiting room they were "hanging off the chandeliers." As if there were fancy chandeliers in some dingy audition hall. I think I get a lot of my euphemisms from my mom, as she had a great way of analogizing and describing things. But there we were. And my dirt-poor mother was thinking I had no chance in hell at landing this gig and bringing in some extra money for us. She worked two jobs already, and we were struggling, which is why she brought me to this crazy place to begin with.

So apparently, when I went into the room, all the people, the director and the casting agents, were sitting around, and I was not unlike the puppy that they brought in. I was being observed, and the goal was for them to choose me and take me home! So I started playing with the puppy. Standard fare, probably not too different from what the other babies who didn't totally freak out did; and just then, when they were chalking me up as another decent non-flipping-out child, the dog bit me. Everyone stopped! Oh shit!

My mother said she could see the word "lawsuit" on every-one's frozen and horrified faces. The room went and stayed silent. I looked at everyone, probably more scared by the looks on their faces and the energy that hung sour and perilous. The air was thick with fear and anticipation—what was going to happen to the baby who just got bit by that damn dog???? That moment of purgatory was probably when I realized in my eleven-month-old soul that you could conduct the energy in a room, because what I did next was throw my head back and laugh!

As everyone started to actually breathe again, they took my cue supposedly and started to clap and cheer too, again probably out of sheer relief that I was not hurt and taking them to court, and my mom said that they all started animatedly talking to one another and slapping knees and wiping foreheads. Needless to say, I got the job. And my budding commercial and TV movie career began.

Now, it was not all throwing-back-heads-and-laughing moments. I quickly learned that this was a cattle call business and you win some and you lose some. There were rooms of nice people, and rooms that just wanted you in and out. Then there were rooms where no matter what little vaudeville act I pulled out of my hat, they were not amused and I clearly wasn't what they were looking for.

But the worst kind was the room where I could tell I did well, but at the end of the day, there was just someone else who did better or was more right, and I would go home feeling so high, and yet I would get the call that the part was going to someone else and they just said, thank you anyway. For a kid those are hard calls—rejection is a lesson you usually learn later in life. But my mom would take me to McDonald's or something and I'd feel better. Come to think of it, it's probably why I associate healing pain with delicious fatty foods. It really does work!

Back in this moment, though, I wondered which way the pendulum would swing. I could tell I'd done well, but how well? Eventually they turned back to me and asked if I would come back.

Steven said I would have to go on tape this time, and I was like, whatever! If I had to hang upside down and rip out my own nails to do this all over again, I would. I hope I didn't actually put it that way, but that was how I felt. Again, I was a hyperimaginative kid with nothing to lose!

And so I came back. In fact, Steven kept having me back again and again. Each time I felt more like the Fonz and less like a scared kid. There must be something I'm hawking that he likes! I was excited and encouraged. The final audition, he wanted to see if I could scream. I probably said something to the effect of "watch this"; again, I was much cockier at six than I am at forty. And so they turned the tape on, and I watched the wheels of the audio record go round and round, and I waited for Steven's signal. He did and then I did. I screamed. I screamed so loud that I broke the device and the tape stopped.

Again, the room went silent. Oh God. Had I done something wrong? Was I screwed? Would they all turn to each other in a good mood, or was this my lead into the "thank you, but no thank you" phone call? Steven smiled, and that was it. A few days later, the phone call came from Marci to my mom, and my mom told me, "You got the job!" We would start in a few weeks.

I froze. And then I ran to my room and looked at all my poster friends on the wall. Kiss and Blondie seemed especially "hats off to you" with their tongues out and rocker hand gestures. Superman seemed like a proud puffin, with a "you can do it" look. But

Pippi seemed the most excited. She had that wry smile and that mischievous look in her eye. I felt like I could lift a horse in that moment just like her!

When we got to the first day, I went through wardrobe fitting, and they showed me this tiny little dressing room that would be mine, my little home for the next three months. We were at Laird Studios in Culver City, which was the old David O. Selznick studio. It was quaint and more intimate than other studios. Instead of trailers you had bungalows. And then they led me to a little schoolhouse, and they said I would start to clock in my three hours a day, which is the requirement today. Under child labor laws, anyone under sixteen must attend three hours of school a day and work no more than nine and a half hours—a rule I sorely miss as an adult when I am on set in the seventeenth hour of the day and still going. I will sit on set and mutter under my breath when I see children being let go—"Friggin children's hours! Ha!"—because now I just want to go home!

But back then you would have to pry me away. When my time was up, I was devastated. Depressed all the way home, only to wake up and run back! And that was what we did. Every day my mom would drive me to work, and I would go into the little schoolhouse and join all the other kids.

Now the kids on this film were Henry Thomas, who played Elliott, and Robert MacNaughton, who played Michael. I finally had the brothers I had made up in my imagination. They were the best. They teased me just like an annoying little sister, and I had never been happier.

Then there were the "D&D boys," which was the name of their gang in the movie, which came from the game Dungeons & Dragons. They were Sean Frye, C. Thomas Howell, and K. C. Martel. They were super cool and I was in awe of them.

There were also the kids in E.T. costumes, a young girl and a young boy, each about thirteen. They did not have legs, and they walked on their hands instead. The tone was that they were like capable superhero circus performers, and so there was no somber attitude. They were part of the gang, and they too were super cool. Matt, the boy, went around with his body on a skateboard and was a total badass, whereas the girl was very sweet and girly, and seemed not one bit different from any of us.

Someone who was different in life, but not in our schoolhouse group, was Pat Bilon, the world's smallest man. He was thirty-four inches tall. And I loved him. I felt like he was a friend just made for me, even though I was fully aware that he was his own person with a full life who went to his own home every night.

We were all like misfits from the Island of Misfit Toys. Or maybe I pictured us more like the *Wizard of Oz* gang, the ones who played the munchkins and apparently wrecked the Culver hotel, which was a block away, while shooting! (A visual that always makes me smile!) I like to think of us as them! We would get in crazy food fights in the commissary, one of them started by

Steven and me! We would play games, make bets, and just hang. One day, on Halloween, we all got dressed up over our costumes. I was a gypsy, and Robert MacNaughton was Nixon, and Henry was a clown. But we all were hearing rumors that Steven, the biggest kid of all, the most playful, the most unpatronizing leader, was about to show us all up. We waited. It was quiet in the schoolhouse. We were all doing our schoolwork, and in walks this old lady, and for a second until our eyes adjusted, we wondered who she was. Well, it was Steven, in full drag, and we all jumped up and attacked him! And we escorted him to set, like a moving wave of groupies in Steven's ocean.

To say that we loved him is the understatement of the world. We didn't love him because it was our job. We loved him because he was like Peter Pan. He believed in us. And for the first time in our lives we realized our own potential through him. I have never had an experience like it.

When the filming was coming to a close, I was so upset. We were shooting the end of the film in the rainforest where E.T. is going home. Steven shot most of the film in sequence, something no one has the luxury of doing anymore because of schedules and budgets, which is a complete shame because often now you shoot the end of a film at the beginning or go so out of sequence that you can't find which way is up because you are guessing how you will feel about things after a journey that hasn't yet taken place. Not to mention you work with people in tight chunks rather than the sprawling nature of the months or years the story calls for.

On this movie we got to know each other, bond, become a family, fall in love with E.T. and each other, and so when it was ending it was truly high stakes for all of us. Steven never let us fake anything. Tears or joy or sarcasm. He made us be real! And that incredible film that he made was all there on the day. Very little special effects, considering. We were not acting to tennis balls standing in for an E.T. that would be placed in later by CGI. He was very much there in the room. He was present. I myself knew that he wasn't "real," but it didn't matter. He was alive in the electric sense of the word. I saw the cords coming out of him. I saw kids taking his head off to breathe while in the E.T. suit, but it still didn't shake my belief in him.

In fact, the fact that he wasn't real meant he could keep secrets. And I could tell him anything. I often sat with him alone while the crew had gone out for lunch. I would wrap a handkerchief around his neck and eat with him. I cared for him. I didn't need him to have feelings in order to actually care about his feelings.

So when we were in those woods, saying good-bye, I was a mess. I couldn't stop crying. It was working for the scene because E.T. was going home, and then I got rumblings that they needed another day to shoot. All of a sudden the idea that this would not all be ending as soon as I thought cheered me up so much, Steven came over and told me that I needed to be upset! Not happy! And

I followed instruction, secretly relieved for this not to be going away in hours but days.

When you end a film, especially just as an actor, that's it. You are sent home, back to normal life, as if it was all a dream. *A Boy's Life* was over, and I thought that I would never hear or see anything about it again. Much to my relief, I had become so close with Steven that he accepted my wish, conveyed by my mother, to have him be like a godfather to me. He stepped up to the plate. He took me in, a girl who needed a father, and it meant the world to me. And he was such a good father figure too. Consistent. Caring. Strict. Wholesome. Nurturing.

And most of all it was relaxed and easy. It became normal to spend weekends at his house, and it was the safest place and time I knew. I thank God for his care and guidance because it truly made the biggest difference in my life. And he single-handedly changed my life. And that is the truth, and I was about to find out what that meant.

After months of silence on the film, we heard that the name was going to be changed to *E.T. the Extra-Terrestrial.* OK, great. Then we heard that people were really loving it. It was as if there was some kind of buzz in the air. Again, this was 1982, so you really had to search for your information, but one day on the TV, it showed that people were lined up around the block to see the film, and the ones coming out of the film were crying and full of joy and emotions. It was becoming a phenomenon. Days went by, and then the news wasn't hard to come by at all. *E.T.* was breaking records. Our little experience was becoming a worldwide freak-out!

And so, to ride the wave, the studio sent us all on a world tour! I remember my mom rushing me out of school to go to the federal building to get a passport so that we could travel! My picture was taken in my school uniform, and I had the biggest smile on my face ever. All of a sudden, I was a girl with a stamped passport to my life's wildest adventures. I was in Germany. Norway. Paris. England. I met Princess Diana, and got to present her an E.T. doll. And I looked as any seven-year-old meeting a real-life princess would look. I was trying to keep my jaw off the floor and my eyes in my head. I loved her. And Steven made sure I bowed properly as I handed her this token stuffed animal.

The last stop on the tour was Japan! That was the world that seemed the most exotic and far away from where I lived. However, Steven had been versing me on sushi all summer, so I was excited to eat the food. Steven loved to freak people out with food, hence the food fights, or he had a game called "see-food": He would put food in his mouth and then open it and say "See food!" and we all howled! He would dangle clams and then slurp them, and we would all yell "Gross!!!!!" and he loved it.

But here in Tokyo, Steven was bragging to me he would eat anything at the sushi bar. While we were eating at the Okura hotel, the sushi chefs overheard him and said, "We hear you will eat anything?" as they laughed, and Steven proudly said yes and took the challenge. All of us kids egged him on, so he waited as the chefs said they had something special just for him! After a minute or two, they brought out a giant five-inch-long centipede-looking creature with several legs, and it crawled across the sushi bar. All the chefs laughed and said, "It's called the dancing shrimp, and you eat it alive!" We all screamed, and for the first time Steven looked like the tables had truly been turned on him! But he ate it, and I got so freaked out I ran out of the restaurant. He had to chase after me, still chewing on the live creature, struggling to get it down his throat.

Each country had a world premiere, and each seemed crazier than the next. Something had crossed over and my not-so-simple life would be even less simple now. Nothing would be simple. But my love and relationship with Steven has always stayed the same. I have always tried to be my best in his eyes. Even when I went through hell, and I was too embarrassed to face him, he didn't judge. He always encouraged me to be my wisest and strongest.

We have had many jokes and profound conversations over the years. I trust him with life advice as I still to this day go to him for it. When he holds my daughters in his arms, I don't think there is a prouder moment for me. Because this one man believed in my silly stories, he made me feel like I could do anything. He single-handedly opened all the doors in my life with that one decision of putting me in that film.

It was my duty to not screw up the opportunity he gave me, and although I struggled here and there, my respect for him, and that experience, always kept me humble and focused. I have always been motivated to live the best life I can. The school of *E.T.* was magical. Thank you again, Steven. Always and forever.

Wild child, 1994

BRONCO

My car didn't have a name, per se; it was just a metaphor for my life. "Wild." "Bull in china shop." "Reckless." I was around seventeen and still living in West Hollywood. Going on auditions again while trying to revive my career, but not in any spotlight. It was just me and my Bronco.

The amazing thing about the late '80s into the early '90s was there was no Internet. No digital cameras. If you wanted to share a picture, you would have to go and develop it and then actually go and present it in person. And no one cared. It is the only period of my life where everyone was in their own bubble and widespread voyeurism had not yet come about and the sharing just wasn't there. I picked out my two-ton car with a navy blue bottom and a tan hardtop because it looked like a big box and I liked cars that were high up—short woman's complex—and it made me feel like a badass. I fitted it with a CB radio and an illegal megaphone that came out the front, below the grille, and you could shout crazy things and give people a real jump. I loved it.

Again, I was not in my oversensitive phase where I was worried about where my life was headed. I could be an '80s child-star footnote or something else, for now I didn't know which way it was all going, and for that moment in time only I didn't care. I just loved hanging out with my two best friends, Justine and Mel. Justine and I were roommates, and we had a little house up in the hills. We would go out, party, paint, smoke cigarettes, and take Polaroids. That's what we did. It was Los Angeles, and we had a lot of friends, and all of them were at the beginning of their exciting lives too. Some of the coolest filmmakers and the biggest movie stars would come hang at our house, but they hadn't become those things yet. We were all in the incubation process and in the last carefree times of our lives. We were human Polaroids slowly developing into what other people would see, but for now we were just scrappy kids in no rush to grow up. I would tool around LA in my big Bronco, just going along with the wind in my hair. I don't even remember what I did during the day. Some days the highlight would be staying in the cabin while going through the car wash and watching the soap and bubbles fall down the windshield. It was all a total blur. Nighttime is when everything would come alive as if I was just waiting for the sky to change color and the days didn't really matter. I slept late and I wasn't expected anywhere and didn't really have anything to do. My responsibilities were to make sure the car was filled up with gas and to have a good mixtape in the car stereo.

And so we would drive around, playing pranks on people in the hills. Mel would get on the megaphone and say, "Pull over, pull over. This is the deer patrol and you are endangering them with your driving. Pull over," and the scared driver would comply, and then we would drive by laughing.

What idiots we were. Sometimes I admit I simply would pick up my handheld mic and tell someone that they were just driving like an asshole and to have a nice day. I was merciless on that thing. It gave a driver a voice that we are clearly not meant to have behind the wheel. I bypassed the rules and drove around town like a total jerk, but I was having so much fun. Sometimes we would just catcall boys. Hey, if they can, then we thought we should be able to as well.

One night, on New Year's Eve, we were at a music show on the Sunset Strip—some hipster band, although that term was not yet in full use, but it was a fun riot and I left feeling invincible as one does after a good rock show. I went to get my Bronco out of the parking lot down the street, only to realize it was closed. And I mean closed. Big, giant twenty-foot-high gate with no signs of life. We had more fun parties to go to, and I was not taking this lying down.

Justine and Mel watched as I defied the laws of gravity and climbed the gate and hurled myself over it. I found my car and opened my baby, got in the driver's seat, and jammed it in reverse.

Now, I could have just jumped in a cab. They are all over Sunset Boulevard. But it would have never crossed my mind because my Bronco was my security blanket in the world. I felt safe in this metal box. It was a part of me. Life wasn't fun without my Bronco.

And so I drove it slowly up to the gate. I saw Justine and Mel standing, waiting, on the other side with the headlights in their eyes. I knew in my mind we could get out of here. That giant gate was in no way going to hinder me taking my car and continuing our evening. I stared at the gate, engine running. I contemplated how I would do this. I deduced that the first step would be to go back as far as I could and then jam into drive. In my vision, I would just hit the gate with one quick slam, like ripping off a Band-Aid, and the force would just pop it open. It would be quick and precise, and that would be that. Bam. Literally.

And so I did. I rolled back slowly with a glint in my eye as I looked out the windshield and zeroed in on my target. I grabbed the steering wheel gearshift and put it into drive. I took a deep breath and jammed on the gas. I knew I would have to slam on the brakes really quick too because once I broke through the gate I would be on Sunset Boulevard in the blink of an eye. So I drove with two feet. As I sailed through the parking lot I got closer and closer, and I asked myself if I should just slam on the brake and call it quits. "No way" was my answer, and into the gate I drove. Justine and Mel looked like they were eating a lemon as they scrunched their faces, awaiting impact. My Bronco went right into the gate with a gnarly metal-tearing crash, and instead of popping it open like a button, my hood forced the bottom of the gate up and it went flat like it was lying down all of a sudden.

OK, now the gate was officially horizontal rather than vertical and I quickly contemplated my next move. A crowd started to gather around to see what that crazy noise was. I quickly jammed it into reverse to get out from under it. I was back at my starting point.

At this moment I should have called it quits, but something took over, and I knew this gate was no challenge for my Bronco and me. I took leave of my senses and went for a second run. When I rammed the gate again, this time the tiny crowd cheered like kids at a party in an '80s movie. The part where someone does something nuts but everyone encourages it. No movement on the gate, however. It was angled ten degrees farther up, looking like someone lying in traction.

I reversed again. The crowd started getting bigger. I mean, it was a bunch of drunken people cruising Sunset Boulevard on New Year's Eve. You couldn't ask for a greater audience to cheer on a crazy girl driving her Bronco through a gate because she had to get to the next party. Another hit! This time the gate looked like it was just falling backward. Of course I couldn't see what my car looked like in front. I just saw the gate was about to go down in this boxing ring. One more giant punch and this thing was hitting the floor with no signs of rejoining the fight. I was irrational and totally without good judgment, let alone any judgment at all.

By this time the crowd was chanting. My girlfriends were just looking at me like they knew I had this in me but this was too far. They were not as crazy as me. I reversed back and took my last big breath. I got the car going by getting the gas pedal down while I still had my foot on the brake so that when I released it, I would be going full speed. I raced forward and took out this motherfucking gate once and for all.

It officially went up over my hood and lay in my rearview mirror on the ground, lifeless and mangled. The crowd went wild. I looked out the windshield to people high-fiving and cheering. Rearview mirror: lifeless gate. Windshield: party. It was a polarity like no other. The cheering eventually died down and people dispersed, going back to their own New Year's world. But no one documented it. I never heard anything about it. It was just a crazy moment that got to be a crazy moment. My girlfriends got in the car and off we went. I didn't know how to feel. The only thing I did feel was pride for my car. I knew we were unstoppable.

The next morning, in the light of day, I surveyed my beloved Bronco. I wasn't a day person to begin with, but this day was particularly bright, and God was showing me what I had done. The damage was really bad. The whole front of the car looked like it had gone through a paper shredder. I felt stupid and embarrassed. Is this who I was? Child-star footnote, here we come. Yikes. I took the car to the dealership, driving into the lot with my head down and my tail between my legs. I didn't have parents to shame me, so

I was doing that to myself. And that really was the crux of the problem. I was still a kid with no guidance. I only had myself.

And that's why I always feel so guilty when I am wrong. Because I am the only person to catch it and make a case for being better. I was at such odds inside myself because I knew there was a part of me that wanted to ram cars and feel invincible. But I also knew there was a part of me that understands there is, at best, a time and place for that. Being an actor, I could fantasize myself into any lifestyle or any person. And at this moment I was in full agreement that I needed a more productive channel than just me and my Bronco. I sat at the dealership, on a hot day in the San Fernando Valley, thinking, I need a new car, and I need a new life.

Self-portrait

THE BLUE ANGEL

There was a club in New York called the Blue Angel. It was in the bowels of the Lower East Side, and my friends and I frequented it. It was a dingy performance-art place with one small stage and soft lighting. My one friend Jon had developed an alter ego as "Dick Haney, the world's worst comedian," and one night, as he was doing a stand-up routine onstage, I spontaneously decided to join him during his set, which was as amateur as anything you can picture. I gave myself the name Lolita and jumped on to the stage. As the bit went on, I was inspired to dance around like an old '60s-movie go-go dancer in slow motion, and take off my clothes, piece by piece, behind him. As this was a place for performance art, I seemed to do just that. At the point when I was like a little wood nymph behind him, we both realized it was time to wrap it up and have the curtain fall. In the snap of a finger it was over and our wild little show was over before it began.

I was in a very free state in my life. This is something I struggle with as a mom because now that I have grown up, I couldn't feel more passionate about being appropriate. Everything in my world is about being "appropriate." People ask me, what are you going to tell your daughters about some parts of your life? I don't want to have to lie, but I am much more invested in telling them how I found my values.

I had to discover for myself what was tasteful or not. I ran through fields and on beaches naked. I was even in magazines in my amazing time of self-discovery. I was posing on the cover of *Rolling Stone* in nothing but a bathtub of flowers. I was working with the most artistic and famous photographers. I thought I was making art. And I was totally in exhibitionist mode without thinking there was a term for it.

In some ways I was just being. I was also playing a bunch of characters, from Poison Ivy to Amy Fisher. One way to escape the child-actress stigma was, ironically, via vixen parts. That certainly changed the perception, all right. Jobs started to roll in after the minor B-movie level of success of those projects. Within a few years I was getting work, but I was also getting typecast. Even in the film *Bad Girls*, my big break back into a studio movie, we played hookers on a mission of vengeance. I wondered where life was going to take me with this double-edged sword of opportunities.

Around this time Steven Spielberg sent a copy of the issue of *Playboy* I'd posed in to my birthday party that had been redone by

his art department. I was now wearing '50s-style dresses throughout the issue, and it was accompanied by a large quilt. The card
read, "Cover up." Yes. I agree. But I had one last stunt to pull, although I didn't know it at the time.

That stunt came after I created my Blue Angel character with
my friend Jon, who, by the way, was a serious intellectual who read
the dictionary so intensely that his dictionaries were the kind of
tomes you had to read with a magnifying glass. Our game with our
group of friends would be to each pick a word from the dictionary
and use it in as many sentences as possible that night. Like, "I only
want to be philanthropic, but oh my goodness, you are so very
misanthropic!" The high-low of our need to stimulate the mind and
yet find silly things to do at night was just a silly juxtaposition, of
course. But we were just kids then. Again, no one had photographed
or documented any of what happened at the Blue Angel, but somehow word had reached David Letterman's producer, and when I
was going on to promote a film, it came up in our preinterview.

His booker said, "Is it true that you and your friend did a show
downtown?" I described Dick Haney and my character, Lolita, and
how silly and quick and crazy it was. So he said, if it was OK, could
I talk about it on the show with David? "Sure," I said. Again, I was
in a very free state and I had always loved David Letterman since
the day he went on the air. I loved people who were smart and
funny. It would become my favorite combination of someone's per-
sonality. So of course I would discuss it with Mr. Letterman.

The night of the show was David Letterman's birthday, which made things very festive. I was onstage and we started talking about the incident downtown. He and I were bantering back and forth. Laughing and having a good time. I felt safe. As I was describing it, I suddenly out of nowhere got the idea in my head to start acting it out. And before I could even think, I was up on his desk. Trust me, had I thought this through, it wouldn't have gone that way. That moment was just one of completely uncalculated silliness that started gaining motion like a runaway train. If I was trying to be sexy or get attention, it would have felt that way. You could see me trying to catch up to the train that was going, and after I was dancing on his desk, I guess I wondered how I could up the ante and strike a finishing moment, and boom! I lifted my top in a flash, only for David, where no one else could see.

I was shocked at myself, and again, feeling like the train was ahead of me, I turned around and threw my arms up in the air and looked to the audience, like *what did I just do? Is this OK? Am I in trouble?* I didn't even know. But then I just thought, it's time to get off the desk and go back to my chair, and on my way there, I grabbed David by the tie and brought him in for a sweet kiss on the cheek. And it was sweet, but the reaction of what he would think of this whole moment hung in the balance. Thank God, he threw his head back and laughed. He let everyone know that it was OK to enjoy the moment and not overthink. This was a true moment of freedom. And it got to be something fun rather than something wrong. Thank you for that, Dave.

When we got in the car after, I realized that this might make waves. I met up with my friends from the Lower East Side, and we watched the show together when it aired that night. As the show started, I said, "Um, so this might be a little crazy," and they asked me why, and I said, "Let's just watch," and we did. As my dance on the desk started to fly, my friends were as shocked as anything you have ever seen but elated, and the whole thing ended in cheers and people saying "Oh my God" and "I can't believe it." They weren't judging me, but they weren't exactly condoning it either. Wow. I had done something really out there by actually putting it all out there. As I watched myself and my friends laughing from an objective perspective, I realized right then and there that this was the end of an era for me.

And so I started my journey into no sex scenes in movies, modesty clauses in my contracts, and a total lack of nudity in any public forum from there on out. And year after year, I became more uptight. One button higher on the blouse, one inch lower on the skirt.

After that, even though it went so well, and couldn't have come off with a better, more playful tone, I decided to take matters into my own hands. I knew that film had been my great opportunity in the past, so I needed to make it my big opportunity again. I wanted to be a good girl, and I wanted goodness to be the theme of my life and my work.

I had a long road in front of me, but I was ready to walk down that ambiguous and unforeseeable path, and do whatever it took to get there. Even if I had to create the path myself. And I will say it was when I found a script called *Ever After* that I knew I was on the right path. This film was a complete spin on the tale of Cinderella. And it started with a woman telling the Brothers Grimm that they got it wrong. That she was actually a strong, bright, amazing woman who captured the heart of the prince with her mind and her strength. She said that she rescued herself, instead of what we have been taught for years, which is that he rescued her.

I fell in love with that story. Rescue yourself? It empowered me more than anything I had ever known. To realize that we can be conditioned to believe that things are one way, and then later be set free to understand they can be different. Fairy tales are also always dark until that light comes and it is earned. I wanted to rescue myself. And I did. I wanted to become a lady. And although it took years, I feel like I did. And I now know how to teach and instill the pillars of wholesomeness. And that it doesn't have to be boring. You can be a warrior and be full of grace and class. That being free is about freeing yourself. In full clothes, of course. Corset, chastity belt, and a full turtleneck.

Nancy and Chris, 1999

FLOWER LIFE

One of the questions I get asked most, other than "Why are you so much shorter in person?," is "How do you do so much?" First, thank you for even thinking I do, but if I actually do, I believe it's because of the people I work with at our company, Flower.

The thing that was so revelatory about Flower, which began as a film company but became so much more, was that by creating it, I was also building a family. It was also about learning that you do absolutely nothing on your own. By yourself, you are just a solo daydreamer. But with a partner or a team, you are unstoppable. I have worked with Nancy Juvonen for more than twenty years on all the films we have produced. And almost every morning of my life, my first call is to Chris Miller, our other partner. He and I have worked together side by side for seventeen years. And I cannot imagine life without either of them.

We are all multitaskers and doers. We can spin plates, and yet much like Nan, Chris always keeps a level head. I have learned so much from them about "reaction" or "how to handle things" or "perspective." If Nan is my sister, then Chris is my brother. When I first met Chris, I knew I met someone as prolific as I wanted to be, and we also happened to share a sense of humor. Chris and I are of a similar age, and so all our cultural references are the same. From old commercials to *Mommie Dearest* and *Pretty Woman* quotes. We work long hours, but we are laughing most of the time, and that's where my other valuable lesson came from: to feel blessed and recognize that working with people you like will make you want to work more! Everyone wears many hats and we all like to do many different things at our company. We all dream stuff up, but more important, we find ways to make it a reality. We say to each other, "What about this?" And if we like it, we figure out a way to do it.

We started out in 1994 as Flower Films. We wanted to produce movies. For three years, we didn't officially contribute but were allowed into the process on four films (*The Wedding Singer, Home Fries, Scream,* and *Ever After*) so that we could really learn how to do things with the greatest effectiveness as producers. It was invaluable, and we were grateful everyone was so open with us.

Then we got to make our very first film, which was *Never Been Kissed.* And we labored over every little detail and could not have been more invested, and we put so much love into every minute of it. It worked well for the studio, but mostly we were relieved by the success because it meant we got to do it again. Next we tackled

Charlie's Angels, then *Donnie Darko*; *50 First Dates*; *Olive, the Other Reindeer*; *Duplex*; *Music and Lyrics*; *Fever Pitch*; *Whip It*; *He's Just Not That into You*; and more to come. We just tried to make stories that we really personally enjoyed and believed in. We kept our heads down and always tried to let the work speak for itself. To us that was everything.

Eventually we actually made our employers an accumulation of almost a billion dollars. Which was, once again, a relief. We wanted them to be as happy as we were for believing in us.

Now we work a little less, due to having families, and we work on different things other than films as well, like all things "Flower."

Flower Beauty, a company I started five years ago, is my main focus these days. I get to work all day right now at a job that is romantic in its art of creating pigments and innovations for color cosmetics; we scour the country going to all the different labs in search of the latest innovations for our line, and yet it satisfies my business side as well, because I am a part of the function and success of the brand. We also make fragrance and eyewear, and are expanding categories by the year. Most important, I run all the advertising, marketing, and publicity, so that makes me think all day long about what women need and how to make them feel good. Positive images and messaging. I come from a storytelling background and I learned so much about marketing as a producer.

I love multigenerational brands. I now think about Chanel, Esteé Lauder, and Clarins, brands that have families running them.

I want my daughters to run this company if I have earned the right to keep it going! It's for women by women, and it is a healthy mind-set and life to bring my girls up in. I also can work from home sometimes and wake my kids up, spend most days with them, as well as do dinner, bath, and bed. I am a traveling salesman at times, but nothing that truly keeps me away. I have found a profession that is conducive to my life now, in this most important chapter!

Maybe I feel like I can do many different things because all my life I played characters that did different things, so that kept my mind open to fantasize. I try many other things. Photographer? Why not? I have taken pictures for the past twenty years; sure, I can shoot the cover of that magazine or publish a book of my photos. Write books? Why not? It will only take me a solid focused year of working on it every day, but yes! This needs to come out of me. So yes! I can do this. Make wine? Chris and I traveled for seven years trying to upstart our label, and here we finally are—we make wine with the Jackson family and travel the country to get it out there.

I have an insane work ethic! I am strict with myself. I'm trained to work. I don't know life without it. Work takes giving it your all, or it will not get done right. You have to kill yourself. Do your homework. Exhaust yourself. Focus on every detail. You have to put all of yourself into something with your heart and your gut instinct, your personal taste and your belief, or it will not get done right. Which can lead to failure. Even if that failure is just knowing that you cut corners. And that is not an option.

Again, I don't know where my motivation comes from. My parents were both hippies who really did not perform on any level. Whose genes am I pulling from? Ironically, Chris and I both come from single-mother homes that did not have privilege on the outset. For me, whatever I lacked in stability or tradition was replaced by a great instinct of who to follow. Nan has lived all over the world and is adventurous, and Chris is up for going anywhere we need to be, geographically speaking. Due to being someone who started my own adventures so young, I recently calculated that I have lived in approximately fifty different cities, states, and countries for work or life, so I am also open to going anywhere. Mason Hughes, a gentleman at Flower, he and I have a saying... "You never know where the day is going to take you!" and it's true. One day we are with a Chicago sales team for wine, the next we are in Fayetteville, Arkansas, for an optical lab visit for our Flower Eyewear line at Walmart, and the next may be deep in Oxnard, California, at a laboratory, looking at the latest developments in skin care. Then one day I might find myself in New York at none other than Penguin Books, with my editor, Jill (love her!), finishing the final touches on this book. A book I had wanted to write for seven years, but it was never the right time, until now.

So when I call my fellow Flowers some mornings, I love that ideas are welcomed. We may not be able to do them all, but it is a safe place to dream. And sometimes, if you really work hard enough, dreams come true.

Australia, 1998

ADAM

When I first met Adam Sandler, I was in my early twenties. I met him at a coffeehouse in Hollywood because I begged, borrowed, and stole to get him to sit down with me. He was very popular from *Saturday Night Live* and from his films *Happy Gilmore* and *Billy Madison*, the latter of which was directed by my friend Tamra Davis, who confirmed he is such a good person, which is everything.

I was convinced at the time we were supposed to pair up. I knew it. I knew it in my bones. I thought Adam had a goodness that was so unique. I could tell that he possessed something different, and I was so drawn to his light. I wanted to make love stories, but I wanted them to have a certain energy that was about true love and chemistry and timelessness, and I was convinced of us doing something together.

When I finally got to meet him, I showed up in a long vintage leopard coat with jet-black hair, pink plastic high heels, and groovy sunglasses. Adam was in sportswear. Cargo shorts. T-shirt and baseball cap. It was definitely not obvious we were supposed to fit as well as I believed because we looked like a preppy and a punk set up on a bad blind date. But I shook his hand with fervor, thanked him for meeting me, and began to plead my case to him.

I told him that, for whatever reason, I knew that we were supposed to become a team. I said we both have production companies and clearly like working with people we trust and want to find our own material. He wrote and I didn't, but I said I had some ideas for films, and if he had anything written, would he consider seeing me in it and tailor-make it for us? It was bold, but I have always been a "you only live once, so let your love show and take risks" kind of person.

He liked my pitch and I had planted my seed. I was happy, and I told him I would follow up. We hugged good-bye and then he told me he was having a party so I should come by, and I apprehensively did. His party was really fun and lots of people were there, but I wasn't a big Hollywood social type, and I made a mental note right then and there that I didn't want to be seen as another party girl to him. I knew we were destined for something meaningful, and dating and socializing were not what I was after.

Months later I would check in here and there, send him scripts with a question mark on them, and one day he called me. He told me he had the idea of a movie about a guy in a wedding band and that there was a script, but it would have to be completely rewritten.

So I came on board, and we got Carrie Fisher to write the girl's part to make it balanced. Frank Coraci was the director, and I just knew he had everyone's back and I loved him. Then Adam and Tim Herlihy, his longtime writing partner, did their pass again because the whole first script was theirs, and then they got their friend Judd Apatow to write on it, and after all these cooks came in, well, it was so good I couldn't take it. And lo and behold, we were off to make a movie called *The Wedding Singer*.

We had the most fun making it you could ever imagine. And I promise you can tell when people are having fun. It comes out through the celluloid and onto the screen, and it cannot be disguised. Adam's friends who are his team were the best, and I fell in love with all of them, including Allen Covert, an actor, writer, and producer who is in all of Adam's movies, and Jack Giarraputo, his producing partner. We played, we partied, and we became real, no-bullshit friends.

When the film came out, we all rented a bus and went around New York stopping at every movie theater we could. We would run off the bus, buy tickets, run in, watch five minutes of the film in whatever part it was in at that moment, and then scream, run out, get back on the bus, blast Daft Punk's album *Homework*, and go to the next stop, all while dancing the entire way!

At the end of the night, when we got to Elaine's, a New York institution, the whole studio was there celebrating, looking at the weekend numbers as they came in, and it was all smiles. The movie was going to be a hit.

And as relieved as I was, I was just happy that Adam believed in me that day at the coffee shop and found us the perfect film to make. I wanted us to be like an old-fashioned movie couple. He was my cinematic soul mate. And maybe I had just proved it to him tonight.

Many years later, we remained friends. We always talked about doing something again, but our lives had moved on in many ways, and we were not actively pursuing anything. However, I knew that we were always subconsciously looking for things as we read them. But for me it was going to have to top what we did, and that wasn't coming easily.

One night, my partner Nan—of course, as she always found the best projects—came and brought me a script. I was busy making a movie with Penny Marshall called *Riding in Cars with Boys* at the time, and Nan wanted to make this film right away. She said we could just produce it and find another actress. I said sure, why not? Then she asked me if we could stage a table read, and I would read the girl's part and we would get someone to read the boy's. It would help her hear the script so that she would know who to suggest for casting when she tried to go and secure the rights to the script. So we did.

And as I read this script out loud, I realized why she loved it so much. It was a drama that took place in Seattle, and it was about a girl who lost her memory every day. But the guy would try to help her remember who she was. It felt small, deep, and very emotional. But above all, it was beautiful and romantic. I told Nan that she had to go and secure this film immediately.

A few weeks later she called me: "They are giving the script to someone else, another company, and they won't say who." I was sick. There was something about this film that had lit a fire in me that not only wouldn't extinguish, it burned brighter by the week. I followed it like a hawk. And it very much did go to other people. It kept traveling. Going from production companies to different filmmakers. They even attached other actors at one point.

But I never gave up tracking its every move. There were huge movie stars and big-time directors attached to it, so it was very hard to even try to get it back. A few years later I found out, once again, it had changed hands. Wondering who got to have it this time, and seeing if there was once again a window for me and Nan to get back in, even though it was never ours, I found out that it had gone to none other than Happy Madison, Adam's company. OK. I knew what I had to do.

I sat down at my old Olivetti typewriter. Funnily enough, I was working on the Sony lot, making *Charlie's Angels: Full Throttle*, and his office was there, only a few hundred feet away. But I started typing nonetheless. And it was like conducting a symphony. The tears in me started to swell as I wrote about my history with this script. How long I had loved it. Why I loved it. How I truly felt once again in my bones that I was supposed to have something to do with it.

And that the fact that it was with him, well, this was a film worthy in every way of our reteaming, and would he please consider doing this with me? Crying, I typed, "This is it. This is the one, I know it!" I hoped I wasn't being presumptuous, but I meant it when I said to him, we need to make more movies. I took the letter, folded it up, put it in an envelope, and had it hand-delivered to his office. I counted the minutes and hours until I heard a response. It was like waiting to see the lighthouse in a storm. I awaited some kind of closure or my fate.

Adam walked over from his office to our trailers at *Angels* base camp. He said, "Of course we can do this! But we want to turn it into a comedy," and I said, "That's fine, but it can't lose its romance," and he said, "I know what guys want," and I said, "I know what girls want," and he said, "Well, then why don't you produce it with me?" and I said, "That's what I was hoping you were going to say," and I jumped into a giant squeezy laughing hug with him! Happy Madison and Flower Films!

I was able to tell Nan that we were going to get to "tell this story," as she always said. And so we did. We immediately went into meetings to take this drama into a more comedic world. Adam, Allen, Tim, and Jack were all there. All the same people we worked with on *The Wedding Singer*. Adam is loyal and consistent with his team. As am I with Nan and Chris. So we all feel like family. We get how important respect is and we all love each other.

One day Adam said, "Instead of Seattle, how about Hawaii" for where the film would take place. And we all screamed, "YES!"

Then the next day I would hand in a set of notes that all said, "Let's discuss," after each draft of the script came in. Because you really don't know what's going to work or not until you try it, especially with comedy. You have to not hinder that process.

Nan and I would really fight for aspects of the love story, and it was a tricky one, because you're dealing with daily memory loss—something that seems so otherworldly—and how that logic feels without losing the magic. It was a very interesting tone we were all trying to weave together. Nonetheless, we all went off to Hawaii, and we had as much if not even more fun than we did on *The Wedding Singer*.

A few days into shooting, I thought, this is paradise, and I just wanted to stay here forever. I have had a lifelong love affair with Hawaii, but I had never worked there. Cameron came to visit me; she wanted to escape a little, so she got the hotel room next to mine, and we had a little middle living room in between. Adam introduced her to his surfing instructor Hans, and when I would leave in the morning for work, she would grab her board and go surfing.

Then we would all meet up at the end of the day. Our two friends—Lona Vigi, who does hair, and Robin Fredriksz, who does makeup on many of Cameron's and my films, and are part of our "girl group"—worked on the film as well, and obviously Nan was there, and let's just say that for three months, life was perfect. Cameron decided to stay a little longer, then she never left, so we rented a Ping-Pong table to put in our living room, and it turned into headquarters. All the guys would come over and play. It was fun, wholesome, communal, and a moment in my life that felt so safe I can't even begin to do it justice.

And we were making a film I truly believed in, and the message of the film is "How do you make love stay?" Because it doesn't matter if someone has a memory or not, you have to reinvent love every day. It's why I chose the book *Still Life with Woodpecker*, by Tom Robbins, as the book my character, Lucy, reads every day, because that book asks that question and then goes on a wild ride just like the film. Love is the one uniting, relatable thing in everyone's life. It's what we all want and struggle with and fight for. And I loved the version of that we were telling here, in paradise.

We decided to open the film on Valentine's Day, which is when we put *The Wedding Singer* out, so we thought, stick with tradition. I was hosting *Saturday Night Live* again, and because Nan and I were producing this one, I wasn't as carefree about the weekend as I was with *The Wedding Singer*.

Weekends have become so important that it is very stressful, and you lose some of the feeling of what you intended, because it's business at the end of the day. Did it work? Will you get to do it again? Those are always my questions because those are the facts.

So I didn't want to know what the money numbers were until Monday. I wanted the weekend to be pure and for the movie to just be what it was, a story I really wanted to tell. But Adam showed up at *SNL*, his stomping grounds. He came into the dressing room with the whole gang, Allen, Jack, etc. I looked up at him. He knew

I didn't want to know. We made small talk, but the cloud of success or failure hung in the air like a giant thunderstorm that would strike me dead or be the rain dance of joy.

I knew by the look in his eye that he knew what I didn't want to know yet. But he couldn't help himself: "Don't you wanna know?" His face was pokerish enough that I said, "Do I want to know?" with a face that just ate a lemon. "Forty-five million. We just broke records"—and the whole room started screaming. And I started doing my rain dance and we all celebrated. This was one in a series of perfect moments. And above all, I was relieved.

Years later, I called Adam one afternoon and said, "Can you meet me for lunch?" and of course we did sometime the next day. We talked about how it had been another ten years again—twenty in total since *The Wedding Singer*—and should we find something again? Adam has two daughters now, Sunny and Sadie, and I had my little Olive. We ate burgers and talked about what to do next, and that we would go on the hunt again to find something. And we hugged good-bye on the street. A few months later Adam found *Blended*, a film about the modern state of families. Now that we both had kids, I liked telling a story about, literally, families and what that means and "what kids need" and "what kind of parent do you want to be?"—all of those themes had never been more important in my life, and it just came together, and our Frank Coraci, who did *The Wedding Singer*, directed it, and it felt like home.

We were off to Africa, and we all brought our families and

made the film. I took Olive on safari almost every weekend and just made an amazing life experience and adventure out of it all. I knew that my film life was winding down, the hours are so hard with kids. But with this group, the balance was there. I can be a mom and work because they celebrate their wives and their kids. It is very conducive to real life, and not all films are like that. But this was, and once again, we just had a wonderful and cozy and fun time making the film.

At the end, we went to Georgia to shoot the part of the film that doesn't take place in Africa. We all lived on a lake, which is my favorite thing in the world, and after work I would go and kayak by myself and take in my whole new life. I would acknowledge how I felt different. All that passion and drive I used to have toward movies was now dedicated to my kid, and yet I was still lucky enough to do all of this with old friends.

This odd man across the lake from me blasted "Rainy Night in Georgia" on a loudspeaker, and I just became still, right there in the middle of the water, happy with where my life had taken me.

As we were preparing ourselves for landing after another round of very epic months of being together every day, we came to our last day of shooting. Adam and I had made another movie, and we just hoped people liked it. I was content. Calm. Happy. And then came the best news ever: I found out I was pregnant. I was going to have another baby. It was the perfect moment to be introduced to the notion of Frankie.

So our film ended, and my new adventure began. And I was amazed that Adam and I both have two daughters. It's incredible how life works. When Adam and I met, we were basically kids. But now we were in the same place in our lives again, but a very different place from where we started. We're not all playing Ping-Pong. We are going to our kids' birthday parties. Adam's beautiful wife, Jackie, and I talk about being moms, and that's the conversation.

Recently, at Adam's daughter Sadie's birthday party, Adam and I found ourselves in a corner. "What are we going to do next?" I asked. "I don't know. I have some ideas," he said. Then I turned to him and said, "Maybe it should be something really crazy? And different?" But then I thought about the heaviness of a drama, and would that make people happy? I don't know. Then I said, "Well, whatever it is, it's gotta be good!" and he said, "We'll find it." We both joke about how old we are going to be in the next one. We both are truly dying to remake *On Golden Pond* because it takes place on our favorite lake in New Hampshire, funnily enough right where Adam and Nan both grew up. Small world.

I think we also like the comfort of thinking we will be together when we are really old. Whatever it may be, and wherever it takes place, I know this . . . I once knew a boy named Adam. And I hoped that we could be a team, but what I found was a true partner. I now know a man named Adam, and trust me when I say, he is as great as you want him to be.

Steven and me, 1981

THE ACTING LESSON

I learned the two most important things about acting by the time I was six.

From 1976 to 1983, while my mom was trying to become an actress, she had us hanging out at the Strasberg Institute in Los Angeles. Lee Strasberg was one of the most important and famous acting teachers ever to live. And he and his wife, Anna, were running the school. He had taught everyone from Al Pacino to James Dean, Dustin Hoffman to Marilyn Monroe, and many other icons of our time. Anna would soon become my godmother, at my mother's request, a relationship that would become so important to me as a kid because she was so kind and so nurturing. She put the mother in godmother, and helped shape me for the next seven years, mostly by just letting me live in her home and feel safe.

Anna's home was like a beautiful commune in that the door was always open and people were always coming in and out. There was every famous actor you could think of and great writers and directors. It was a salon type of place. There would always be several people watching movies or sitting in the living room, having conversations. It was truly the most fluid, creative energy I had ever seen in a house. It was like a stimulating heaven. There were also Anna's two sons, Adam and David, who became like big brothers, and they helped me not become a wuss and turned me into a bit of a tomboy, which I greatly appreciated.

Some nights, after Lee passed away, I would crawl into bed with Anna and she would just let me sleep. It was so peaceful, and I felt like nothing bad could happen there. Anna had lost her soul mate, Lee, and I could not imagine what that feeling was like. I couldn't actually fathom it yet. But what I did see was that life went on in this house. And I mean LIFE. The house literally buzzed. It glowed with love and whimsy and acceptance. A sense of family. This home formed me, but not until many years later would I try to replicate it. Now I have a beautiful welcoming haven myself. Anna taught me this.

Back in 1979, my mother was doing a play at the Strasberg Institute called *Playing for Time* about women in a concentration camp. My mother was playing one of the women in the camp, and they ended up giving me a small part as well. I was to play a girl who walks across the stage and says good-bye in German as she is taken off to be executed. I had two words to say, *"Auf Wiedersehen."* And then I waved and that was that. So absolutely heartbreaking but important was this play. These stories needed to be told. The lead actress, who carried us through the story, was a tall, androgynous woman who had to be in the greatest turmoil throughout the whole play, every night. Crying, screaming, fighting for her life.

I didn't know how she did it. I was in awe of the fact that she could be this emotional every night. What did she do to prepare? What was her ritual and where did she go? So one night, I started looking.

I would walk through the darkened theaters that were empty, with all the ropes and curtains. I would follow the cables on the floor that wound around like snakes as they powered the bright lights that would illuminate the actors. These rooms were scary at night. Hundreds of empty seats. Ghosts and dust. A silence that felt like something could jump out and come alive at any minute— think the-anticipation-of-a-giant-jack-in-the-box feeling. When a play is going on, it is alive. Now this theater was just a den of secrets waiting to be let out. But I braved these rooms in search of the crying woman.

And then one night, I found her. I had gone into a different little theater in the building, and I hid behind a curtain so she could not see me. She was just lying down on the stage with her legs dangling off the edge. Crying. And she would beat her chest and conjure up these monumental tears. Then it would subside a little. Then she would beat her chest again, and moan as if she was dredging up the ocean floor of her own personal painful memories. And like the waves, her sobs ebbed and flowed from loud war cry to vulnerable smaller tears. And I realized that when she went out there every time, when she entered the stage, she was already in some truthful-beyond-upset, flipped-out state, and that was what she would provide to the audience of people. But it had come from such a private place in her, a place that she had summoned next door.

Now that I knew how to find her, I spied on her, night after night, watching her drum up the pain and start to wail. There were no actor tricks. No stepping into character at the last second. She was willing to unzip herself and get to a truth I'm sure most people would prefer to avoid. She gave herself fully. She intimidated me, but I could not stop watching her.

Lesson one: Make it personal.

I was four years old.

The second lesson came when Steven Spielberg, on the set of *E.T.*, said something to me when I was six years old. He said, "Don't act your characters, BE your characters." I thought back to my nights of watching that woman cry in the empty room. She wasn't acting, she was *being*.

Throughout my career I would play many facets of things I actually experienced in life. It was cathartic and productive. I always had a way to channel things. The first film I did after *E.T.* was *Irreconcilable Differences*, about two parents going through an ugly separation, with lots of family damage. I felt I had a lot to bring to that. Same with all the characters I played. Riot girl, check! Aspiring young woman who wants to rescue herself? Yep. Girl searching for love over and over, check, check! Messed-up woman who struggles to grow up and just wants a little attention—i.e., Edie Beale? OK, we have a few differences. She had a much better fashion sense than I ever have! The truth is, I have never acted a day in my life. I think I would fail miserably at it. And the older I get, the more I have come to terms with so many things that I simply don't have the same drive to get to all the pain. And I think I have tapped into every girl who wants to find love! Now I'm just me. And nobody wants to watch a woman strive to be a normal mother of two. Or maybe they do? Is there enough drama in that? Well, there is, but it might not be as cinematic. And any drama that occurs in my real life, that I struggle with, I prefer to keep it private. So where does that leave me? *Charlie's Angels 3*, anyone?

The truth is, I find acting jobs when something comes along and I can't stop thinking about it. It will keep me up at night! A fire starts inside that I cannot extinguish. I start relating it to my own personal experiences. I start seeing what I could do with it. I actually get territorial about it. Thinking that I could do this because of *X* experience that I have lived through and understand. I can put that circumstance and the feelings I had with it. I can make it mine even though it's in the disguise of someone else.

And maybe now it's about telling the occasional story that I really believe in and think would be good to put out there into the world. But as I look back, that crying woman taught me how to approach everything in life. Acting or otherwise.

Be authentic. Be yourself. And most important of all . . . make it personal.

Flossy

FLOSSY

When I was around eight years old, my mother almost let me buy a dog. It was a black Chow puppy. We were in Los Angeles, at a pet store in the Beverly Center, and I had played with it in the strange room where they let you play slash examine slash bond slash whatever. The room was more like a hermetic fluorescent-lit closet, but I felt nothing but warmth and love. I knew I wanted this dog!!

We were at the register, and my mother was breaking out her checkbook (as that was the modern form of payment then), and as she started writing, my heart started pounding. I started fantasizing... This dog and I would talk, and this dog would be there to listen to me talk about my problems! We could sleep curled up in the bed. We could make it look like life was not so abnormal. We could look like a Norman Rockwell painting. As my fantasies started to drift upward into the sunset, I saw her pen slowly stop writing! She turned to me and started talking about how this wasn't going to work. That "we travel all the time for work"! About how I "probably wasn't ready for the responsibility"! That this whole idea was "bad, impractical, and just not the right timing" because "life was just too hectic"!

You're goddamn right!! It is too hectic! I have been working for the last seven years and I'm only eight! You're nuts, Dad's nuts, and I want a friggin anchor in life! And this pile of fur was going to be that for me!!! How dare you!!!!!! And that check you're writing is technically my money as well. So if we have to saw this dog in half, I am leaving with this Linus-like security blanket of a dog, you heartless tease slash canine cockblocker!!!!!

Sad to say, she was still the adult, and we left that store empty-handed, and I wondered when I would ever right that wrong.

Enter Flossy!

When I was about nineteen, I started thinking that maybe it was time to try again. So I decided that I wanted rescues. Never a pet store again. Even when I set that scarring childhood moment at the pet store aside, it seems crazy to me not to save a life. I knew I wanted two dogs because I wanted them to have each other. So looking for two young rescues began. It took me months and months. After a series of shelters, newspaper ads, and various other sources, I was at the Pasadena City College Flea Market one Sunday, walking around, and there was a playpen of puppies that needed to be rescued. A whole litter! Instead of dropping them somewhere or taking them to a shelter, the owners wanted to try this venue, where they knew a bunch of people would be. There were about fourteen in the litter, and I thought, *Holy cow! Not only could I get two kids that would have each other in this life, but also they could be siblings!!!!!!*

Knowing this was the moment, I looked inside, and there were a bunch of blond and beige pups. They were Lab-Chow mutts that looked like little bears. People were rummaging through them like it was a sale bin of scarves. It was like a squished sea of moving, squirming fish. It was hard to decipher much. And then I spotted this one. I don't know what it was, but my heart just sang. *That's the one! The hero dog!!!!!! That's the little partner in crime I have been looking for!!! My long-lost sidekick!!! I just have to reach in, grab this one, and then find it a counterpart!!!*

As I plunged my hands into the sea of fur, a woman knocked into me, pushed me aside, and grabbed this dog!!!! I gasped. *"NOOOOOOOOOOOOOOOO!"* I wanted to scream!! I wanted to say, "That's my dog!!! I saw it first!!! We belong together! You don't understand!"

She held the dog up and started clinically examining it, lifting its leg, checking the sex, holding it up without supporting its bottom. As she stared at this dog, time stood still. What was going to happen? Should I tell her? Should I strangle her? Was this the Beverly Pet Heartbreak, Take Two???

The whole scene became quiet. I just waited. Watching them

about two feet away from me as fate hung in the slow-moving wind. I felt helpless and freaked. I think I went into some type of catatonic state. After all, I had been anticipating this relationship most of my life.

And then, the sound started to slowly turn up its dial, and the woman turned to me, and held the dog with her arms extended, and looked into my eyes and said . . .

"She belongs to you!"

A smile erupted in all of my being, and I took this puppy in my arms, held her to me, and said to myself, *Thank God!* Then I looked at her and said, "It's nice to finally meet you!" And I was as happy as a human could be. But before the joy lasted for more than a second, my eyes popped open and I thought, *Shoot, I need to grab your mate! The picture in my mind has two of you!*

So I turned back to the playpen. People were grabbing up all the puppies. People were in anarchy for these creatures! You would never know that there was an entire flea market full of treasures anywhere near! This giant box was where all the action was. So I clawed my way back in with my little hero under one arm, and with the free hand I grabbed one of the last dogs. A boy.

With a dog in each arm, I promised the owners I would give them not just a great home but a great life. And I walked half a mile back to my car, opened up the door, and said to them, "Here is the car. Get used to it because we are going everywhere together."

After I put them in the backseat, shut the door, and then got into the driver's seat, I looked back at them, and I said, "Oh yeah, and we are not going to be neurotic either. And we are going to have so much fun it's gonna make your heads spin!" And we did. For the next sixteen years!

Flossy was more Greta Garbo than Lassie. She was an old-timey gal with a flair for the dramatic. Calm as she was, she had a dry delivery about everything. She smiled after long days on the beach. She was able to express contentment, but she did not hop around spastically. That would be beneath her. She had a take-it-or-leave-it attitude, and was a very cool customer. She also looked like a little white bear.

Her brother, Templeton, was a boy and took a while to grow up, but when he did he was a good little gentleman. He was much more hyper and lopsided in his approach to everything, but I proudly took them everywhere off leash, and they were always good. Easy. They got it. One day, a few years later, I went to adopt another dog at the pound. I named her Vivian, and when I brought her home, she smartly walked up to Flossy and rolled on her back with her legs up in the air in the submissive position. *Phew*, I thought, because anyone who didn't kind of bow down to Flossy was going to have a tougher time of it. However, she walked over to Templeton and started pulling on his ear! And that was it. Templeton finally had a playmate with energy and whimsy. Flossy was never going to be that. She was a solo flyer.

So there it was, the four of us, and life was so good. We were pied pipers, and we went all over the world together, from the south of France to Austin, Texas. I actually got a Volkswagen bus, took out the backseats, and just let them cruise about the cabin. We swam in lakes in New Hampshire and oceans in California. We were a family, and when I picked up photography at twenty-five years old, they were my best subjects. They are the celluloid ghosts of evidence of a large chapter of my life.

My life with them was free, and they forced me into the great outdoors all the time, which was good because I had them in some of my most workaholic and prolific years. They balanced my life and grounded me in every way. I always took care of them, usually putting their comfort before my own, and yet these were truly the three easiest creatures you have ever met. Everyone at work loved them too. They were office dogs. Car dogs. Movie-set dogs. You name it. They were such a part of my identity and lifestyle, and I never felt lonely with them. They slept on my bed. We would take long weekends. I would stare into Flossy's eyes and talk to her, and then take a photograph of her blond eyelashes with a macro lens and make a piece of art out of it. Flossy's eyes were so calm and wise. She was an old soul. And without words, she was one of the beings I felt most connected to in my life. If you look, most of the pictures that have been taken of me during that time, these three dogs are in them. To document me was to include them because they were such a part of my life. Flossy has graced numerous magazines, fitting for the reincarnation of Ms. Garbo.

She outlived Templeton, when he sadly died at fourteen. By some strange stomach flip, he went overnight just like that. I had never faced what life would be like without the three of them. Vivian was only thirteen, but she died a few months later. Like a widow who's lost her beloved husband, she went from perfectly healthy to departing this earth within four months. She simply could not live without him, and her health deteriorated rapidly.

We put her down to the sounds of Nick Drake in the garden. We all sat around, and the doctor administered the shot to close her eyes and end her unthinkable pain. We all held her and tried to make it as beautiful and safe as it could be. Everyone who she touched sat hand in hand in a circle around her. I put Templeton's and Vivian's ashes together on a giant rock that goes all the way out to the water in Malibu Beach, where these two ran up and down for thirteen years. They would live forever in a spot that made them happy. Again, all my friends gathered for the ash-throwing ceremony, and as we said our good-byes as the sun set over Vivian's and Templeton's rock, we read the profound eulogy Eugene O'Neill wrote for his dog, called "The Last Will and Testament of Silverdene Emblem O'Neill": "No matter how deep my sleep I shall hear you, and not all the power of death can keep my spirit from wagging a grateful tail." One giant wave came over it as we all were saying good-bye. Was it them? I can only hope . . .

Back at home, Flossy was exercising her third act. Now, as the star of the show, and with no disrespect to her brother and sister, she had the floor and a new glint in her eye. It was by no means evil, just slyly content to have the calm and quiet around her. She could just be as she always was, just an old movie-star diva in her own spotlight. And so, just the two of us now, older, slower, calmer, we both were entering profound phases in our lives.

When Flossy and I came together I was nineteen and very much a kid. However, she taught me how to care for someone and grow in such a way that I could have never become the nurturing person I am today without her. My ability to take care of something and someone developed with her. She gave me so much in return. I was so content with her. I never felt alone.

But now I was thirty-five and Flossy was almost seventeen. I spent most of my days at home with Flossy. I could feel she was winding down. One night I said good night to her—she had recently made a habit of staying downstairs at night. I kissed her good night, and I went up to my room. I woke up the next morning and walked down to where she was. She was facing the other way, and I knew. She was gone. Peacefully in her sleep she went up to the angels, and I held her with tears streaming down my face. There was nothing I could do or say to this fluffy shell that housed a soul that meant so much to me. She had made me whole in this world. My silent partner. My old-world friend.

This was my third time to go through this process, and I had found these wonderful people who come to collect dogs' remains, and also cremate them and give you the ashes in a meaningful dog-themed urn. I held her until they came. I said good-bye one last time and slumped down on the floor. To say I was lost is the understatement of the world. After a few light-headed hours of feeling like I had been staring into the sun, I got an idea. I picked up the phone and called my travel agent, and when she picked up she asked how I was. I burst into tears and told her what happened. I knew she would be empathetic, and she gave her utmost condolences. I said thank you. She asked, "How can I help?" Then I cleared my throat and took a breath and said, "I want to go to India." She asked for my time frame, and I said I wanted to go as soon as Flossy's ashes were back with me, probably in a day. "All right," she said, "let's get a plan."

And so I did. I took Flossy to India and gave her a proper and fitting send-off. The first place I spread some of her ashes was at Gandhi's house in New Delhi. Then I took her to a Buddhist monastery way up in the Himalayas. And third, I put the rest in the Ganges River off a quiet path in the countryside. I thanked her over and over for her companionship. There is a hole in my heart forever since she has been gone. However, I try to make her proud with all the love that I try to give every day to my girls! Flossy was my first girl. And the love I felt for her is one of the best gifts I have ever known.

I took a small portion of the ashes back to that old rock in Malibu. And hopefully the old band is back together. The three musketeers of dogs I felt so lucky to care for. And I did care for them so very much. I have two dogs now. And because of the kids, I fear they get the short end of the stick with attention compared to the red carpet I rolled out for Flossy, Templeton, and Vivian every day of their lives.

Don't get me wrong, there are toys and treats and love all around. It's just a more traditional dog-to-human relationship and not the profound bond I was used to. My whole world was those dogs, and every extracurricular moment was spent conjuring up our next great adventure. I am now turning to my two daughters instead, saying, "What do you want to do today?" with a big smile and a let's-go cadence!

But I love that my girls are growing up with dogs. We have Lucy—the "White Shark," as Olive calls her when we are all swimming—and Douglas, the scrawny, long-legged mutt with the heart of gold. He's neurotic but truly loveable. The house is chaos sometimes when the dogs are trying to eat the kids' food or jumping into the tub with them. But it's worth it. Life with dogs is better. I just wouldn't have it any other way. They say that dogs can give and receive love through their eyes. The unspoken ability to lock in and actually feel love between human and animal is an extraordinary thing. And we shared many looks of love, me and my girl.

Baking, Los Angeles

DOMESTIC BLISS

I am engaged. I am five months pregnant. I can't make pancakes.

On this particular Sunday morning, I woke up a little cranky. I had a huge zit, and my hair was totally damaged from dyeing it blond, not to mention I was wearing farmer jeans due to my protruding stomach. After sitting in the sun, brushing my hair, and petting the dogs, I came into the kitchen and read the *New York Times*. And then I had the bright idea . . .

"I know, I'll cook some pancakes." I had just gotten a new recipe for lemon ricotta pancakes, and I thought this Sunday morning would be the perfect time to attempt it.

Cooking had become my latest obsession. I had traded going out to concerts and late-night dinners for a stay-at-home lifestyle. Instead of running around in my thirties like I was still a teenager, I was settling down with my new garden and my new cookbooks and trying to play the part of the character I have never been able to master ... THE GROWN-UP.

I thought that herb boxes and homemade meatballs were the gateway to maturity. I had an electric pepper mill, which seemed advanced to me! I fantasized about being the woman who could whip up anything in her kitchen.

Instead, I now am stretched over cookbooks with a look of concentration on my face with no freedom in my step, still working out a lot of kinks in my very spotty cooking. For instance, my fiancé is puking upstairs as we speak, and it's from my lemon ricotta pancakes. Here's what happened ...

First I started separating the egg whites. The recipe said to do that, and then whip them into a mountainous shape. So I did. I didn't have a mixer, so I did it by hand and arm. I wanted to cry in pain after ten straight minutes of whipping. But when the liquid started to become peaks, I was thrilled!

Then it said to take four egg yolks ... Fuck! I threw those away. OK, breathe. Just go get four more. I had now murdered almost a dozen eggs. Not ideal, but I obviously hadn't considered the next step enough, so it's my fault. OK, now I had separated out the yolks, and this time I saved the whites. Not going to be a chump again. Will I need them? Who knows, but in a bowl on standby is better than in the trash.

Step two: Add sugar, flour, and ricotta cheese and lemon zest. So I did. I carefully measured everything like a meticulous baker, and I put it all into a bowl, ready to mix. Fuck. I didn't read that you are supposed to mix the egg and sugar and ricotta, THEN add the flour. No wonder this was sticky!

Feeling guilty about wasting food, I realized that I would have to waste four more eggs to get it right, and do it all over. Resigned to the waste, wanting these to be great for my man, I started cracking the eggs.... There were only three. No fourth egg. OK, fine. I would attempt to adjust the other ingredient ratios. Not something I EVER feel comfortable with. Three-quarters is exactly... one egg less or a quarter, what? I didn't know how to measure that. OK, breathe again. Be free, I told myself, it's only pancakes. So I trimmed the sugar. I trimmed the ricotta, and, of course flustered, I just started zesting the lemon haphazardly into the bowl.

I started mixing it with the eggs, and to my surprise it was a good consistency. OK. This was all making sense, and the flour should mix with this nicely to make something that resembled batter rather than mortar. Great.

I poured in the flour, and it started thickening. Then more thickening, then too thick... FUCK!!!!!!!! I forgot to do a quarter less on the flour. I started throwing spoons.

My fiancé at the time, Will, came downstairs, and instead of finding some sexy brunch-making lady, he found a hissing child. "Don't come near me right now," I said. He has the tendency to want to get involved, and that's the last thing I wanted right now.

"I'll be over here," he said as he headed to the couch and started reading the leftover paper.

Standing over the sink, I just felt lost and stupid. I looked at the counters and it was just a giant mess. I sucked in every way and the evidence was everywhere. It was all a sprawling avalanche of every bowl in my cabinet filled with wrong mixtures and flour and spills and splats of eggs and sugar, not to mention the ten spoons and whisks and wooden spoons lying like dead carcasses.

I was going to make this work no matter what. OK. Now what? Well, I heated up the skillet and decided to pour or, better yet, thwack my batter into the pan and start cooking it. At least, I figured, I could get what the flavor profile was trying to reveal. As the butter started melting and the batter started cooking... I could smell something positive. I got a moment of encouragement. Maybe these wouldn't be right, but they might be edible.

Now, I need to mention a side note that the last time I made pancakes for my man, they were old-fashioned, they were blueberry, and they were raw. He was very nice about it. But it was my goal this time to at least take that screwup out of the equation by simply cooking them through.

The bottom was browning nicely on my current pancake, and I flipped it on over. Looked good. OK. Let it cook all the way this time, I said to myself. I did. And then I flipped it onto a plate, poured a little syrup on it, and served it to my little taster. He started on his first bite. I was tense. And he looked up and smiled . . . "It's good." I felt relieved. "And you know I'd tell you otherwise," he said, and it's true, he would.

As much as I want to kill him when he does tell me he doesn't like something, I am always grateful when he does like something because I know it's genuine! And I hate yes-men. I like it real. Honest. Tough love with support! And of course when you earn praise it even feels sweeter than ever! "So, one more pancake?" I wanted to ask, because if he said no, then I wouldn't know what to think. But instead he asked for another before I could even speak, and I started happily slopping some more paste into the frying pan.

On about the fourth one I started really getting it right. Size. Color. Taste. But by then he was full and the best one of the bunch sat there on the plate. I looked down at it with a sense of pride and thought that I would always give him the later pancakes from now on because the kinks will have been worked out and that is the level of service I would like to provide my customers.

I turned around and looked at the destruction I had wrought on my kitchen. And instead of cleaning up, I just sat down for a minute, thinking that this should have never taken so much out of me. Breakfast is not supposed to wear you out both physically and emotionally. But there I was, slumped on the kitchen table. I slowly started reading the newspaper again.

All of a sudden Will got up from the couch quickly and said, "What did you put in those pancakes?" with a very panicked and pained look on his face. Oh God, what have I done? "Eggs, ri-cotta . . ." I started listing things off and then I said, "Nothing bad, why?"

He said, "I think I have to throw up," and he started off to the upstairs bathroom. As I sat there in the kitchen, wide-eyed, I heard a small whisper from the stairs . . . "I think they were . . . raw . . ." His voice trailed off and the door shut behind him.

Well, I think to myself now, domestic bliss may be one thing, but domestic goddess you are not.

Greece, 1995

JUMPING SHIP

In 1982 I met my friend Mel, full name Melissa, at a John Denver celebrity ski tournament in Aspen, Colorado. My mom in classic fashion befriended her mom, and then when we returned back to Los Angeles, where we all lived, she would bring me to Mel's house for a sleepover, and then show up again three days later to pick me up. This happened a lot. But Mel and I stuck together and stayed friends way past childhood. In fact, we are still friends in our forties with kids.

But one day, when I was nineteen, we heard Mel's mom, Barbara, was going on this lavish boat trip through the Mediterranean, starting in Istanbul and making its way to the pyramids. It was a three-week extravaganza, and frankly, looking back, we were not at our most sophisticated yet, but somehow we visualized ourselves sailing through ancient ruins and wonders of the world! Luxury on the high seas? I'm not sure what we were expecting—

steamer trunks and old-fashioned movie moments for me; Mel, I will never know.

Mel is a salty, sharp-witted gal who causes most people when they meet her to leave with their tails between their legs because she is a cut-you-down-to-size kind of person and, even worse, everyone is laughing because she does it with such humorous flair. She has softened in her older age, and she is probably the most sensitive to those she cares for, yet she hasn't lost her edge totally, I'm happy to say. But Mel is also known to stay around headquarters when we travel. She is the kind of person who would fly to New York for the night, go to her hotel room, sleep, and then fly home the next day. She sleeps in late and does her own thing. Yet somehow she's the person you want to hang with. I can't explain it.

So we heard Barbara was going on this exotic expedition and we petitioned her to take us with her. We said we would pay our own way: I had saved enough money, and, well, Mel would be getting it from her parents as her mom's treat. However, Barbara would soon begin to feel like I was anything but a treat for her.

When Mel and I showed up to meet the group, I was at that age where I had just come into my own body, so I was a non-bra-wearing, vintage-clothes-sporting gal who carried a boom box that I had hand-painted rainbows and hearts and clouds on. I showed up with my serape backpack and super-short blond pixie hair, and I was, simply put, a '90s hippie. Mel, dressed in black, always in black, as if every day was a funeral, in about seventy-five-degree heat, showed up at the airport with me, and from the moment we stepped onto the plane, I could see the apprehension in Barbara's eyes. She knew what this trip was for her: a well-deserved lifetime experience at the age of fiftysomething, her kids finally old enough to rely on themselves, and her moment to take a personal break from it all. Enter us.

On board the Lufthansa aircraft headed for Istanbul, we seemed to get the same look from our flight attendant. Skeptical! Don't get me wrong, Lufthansa is a wonderful airline, but in this moment we were being stereotyped as two young A-holes in business class. A kind of "how did you get this seat?" feeling. We just got the giggles, and sometime after takeoff and a few complimentary champagnes, Mel announced to me that she needed to take a "Lufthansa," meaning she needed to have a bowel movement, and the laughter went from giggles to roaring! More sneers from the cabin crew! But you can bank on the fact that we still make the "Lufthansa" joke to this day—again, great airline!

We landed in Istanbul. It was 1994. And again, I was just not dressed for the environment. I immediately realized I had totally misunderstood the dress code. Not that I had anything in my arsenal that would have been more appropriate, but I was having that "we're not in Kansas" moment the minute we stepped off the plane. However, we proceeded outside to meet our greeter to take us to the boat, and as I walked out of the airport, I saw a giant tour bus. What the fuck! I was a nineteen-year-old semi-punk-rock rebel, and I didn't do tour buses. I also started to rapidly clock the people gathering around the bus, and they were all Barbara's age at best. Oh my God. Mel and I had stepped into a senior moment, and we were the black sheep, to put it mildly. Oh my God. So as we made our way to the bus, I was already freaking out in my head. I hated organized things like this. Less corporate and more running-naked-through-fields was my kind of journey, although I did not wish to run naked in these parts. Even I knew that!

We were handed itineraries, and I was looking at this dossier of everything being organized to the minute. We were to be ushered through every port and every destination. More sweat. We boarded the bus. They took us to a hotel to acclimate to the time zone and experience Istanbul as the first marvel of the expedition. OK, great.

As soon as we got to the hotel, I felt freer. For this day, everything was more relaxed and we were able to go through the bazaars and roam around. The senses delighted. Mel and I wanted to wander the marketplaces; Barbara insisted we go look at rugs because she wanted an authentic Turkish rug to take home with her. When you're nineteen, you're not thinking of worldly possessions and anchoring a room with a memory-filled throw rug. You're not sitting with friends telling the story of how you handpicked this out of hundreds of rugs while drinking tea in the back room of a bustling shop. But here we were, me and Mel sitting cross-legged, drinking tea. I just wanted a beer or something fun, but Barbara ordered us tea, and I didn't want to oppose her. Yet.

The man proceeded for about two hours to unfold rugs in a fast fashion. He unfurled hundreds of them. Mel and I started humming circus music just to keep ourselves amused. I could not tell the difference from one rug to another, but there we sat, stuck until Barbara finally picked one. Good! I thought. Now we can finally leave.

I am sure she was having her own thoughts about me, and they started to bubble when we went outside to see the light of day and there was a pigeon park. Of course, at that time I was a vegan animal-rights activist! So when someone saw a rat with wings, I saw a bird of peace! And so I started feeding them, and they were so aggressive that they started to fly onto my arms and hands. I was loving every minute of it! The locals started to gather around, in amazement, I thought, as if I looked like some bird whisperer. Mel said that they were probably laughing at me for being such an idiot to let these diseased things land all over me. This scene quickly turned Hitchcockian, and the spectacle of hepatitis meets inappropriately dressed American girl had the locals in a frenzy. I looked past the crowd to see Barbara's small face in the distance. Yep! She definitely was regretting letting us come.

Day one. On the boat. I came aboard, and the truth was that this boat was beautiful. It was like a cruise ship, slightly shrunken down but very upscale. Since I had paid my own way, I started to feel my own sense of self, and marched right up to my cabin, shared with Mel, and I unpacked, set up my boom box with loads of fresh batteries, and my case of handcrafted hours-to-make mixtapes that all were decorated with stickers and Sharpies, each representing a different mood. There was the Cat Stevens–style one, the Roberta Flack one, and the acid-house remix one. All over the lot and each one ready to spring to life to get the party started or the wind-down winding.

I have zero gifts in the musical arena, but I have never lived life without an eclectic sound track. Life is better with music, although there is a certain class of jazz I still cannot eat to. It's too energized and spastic and not meant for digestion but more a birthing of the deepest inspiration and a voracious call of the wild. I bring this up because I was becoming that for Barbara. I was quickly becoming something she could not digest to, and when I came into a room, it was as if aggressive life-altering jazz kicked in at level five. We would get to ten soon enough.

We set sail, and I threw on my new white 1940s ruched old-fashioned one-piece bathing suit I bought for the trip and went up to the pool and ordered a froufrou cocktail. I knew they wouldn't question my age because it was more a marvel to them that I wasn't in my golden years like the other passengers. It was more, Oh my God, she's young, rather than Wait, are you old enough? And so with that cocktail cherry being broken, I decided that drinking was going to be my lubricant into total toleration. Turning to Mel with my drink, I said, "This isn't so bad?" Mel and I cheersed as we left the first port!

We sailed all night, and into the dining room we went for our first dinner. This was a serious white-tablecloth atmosphere. Again, I had on a bright paisley Pucci-like dress, unlike the elder ladies of the boat. Oh my God, this is going to be a long trip, I started to feel again as Barbara walked in with her very sensible outfit, which resembled one large pashmina, and we all sat down. We were to eat at this table every night for the next three weeks. So when conversation ran out in the first five minutes, I excused myself and went walking around.

And much to my surprise I found a little casino room! Drinking and gambling, yes, please! So from then on I ordered one course for dinner and made my way out early every night and started hanging with the guys at the blackjack table and the roulette wheel. I felt much more at home swapping stories with this diverse younger crowd, and I didn't feel judged. We actually all had interest in hearing each other's stories. Not to mention I am a gamer through and through. It passed the time and was much more fun than staring at our plates in the dining hall.

One of our first stops after days at sea was the Greek island Crete. The beautiful Mediterranean landscape truly spoke to me. I loved it. I looked up high on the mountain and saw the white buildings. And the color of the sea that cannot be described in the way that it is light and dark all at the same time! It sparkles. It beckons. It is majestic. Today's activity was to get to the top of the mountain where the actual town was and go walking around, shop, and go see ruins. It was like following a herd while a woman told you the history of this and that as you flocked together. No free-form.

I started to grimace. When we all waited to get up to the top, I saw people mounting donkeys and starting their way up the winding hills. What? I was too much of an animal lover to make this poor old donkey schlep my ass up this giant mountain. So, concerned for this creature's well-being, in protest, I said I would walk it. Barbara rolled her eyes, embarrassed that I would not just follow protocol, and as I started up the mountain, the guys shouted, "Miss, it's too far, you must ride the donkey!" I looked back smugly—"I'm good!"—and I mumbled to Barb that I would see her at the top. She responded by giving half a head nod, as if to answer and yet not let on to anyone else she knew me.

Now, where was Mel, you ask? On the boat. Once again, in classic Mel fashion, she chose to sit this one out. She said there were many Greek islands to stop at and she would see one, but for now she felt like just staying in. It didn't surprise me, and yet somehow it was forcing Barbara and me together more and more. Without the Mel buffer it was not fun for either of us. Even though Barbara had known me my whole life, I was at that yucky age for her and she was not at an age for me that I could relate to. We were at a biological impasse here in the islands of Greece. She mounted her donkey and passed me on the way up. I gave her a halfhearted wave.

About an hour plus later, I reached the top. Now I understood why they have guests ride the burros. My legs were simply jelly. They were so shaky that I could barely walk, and this was the start of the day when we were all supposed to walk around for hours. Oh shit. I limped around in pain and counted the minutes till we could get back on the boat and I wouldn't have to look interested in what our guide had to say. All I wanted to do was break off and go sit in a café and see local culture. But I went with the flock and to Crete school we went.

Luckily I found a gondola that went down the mountain in another area, and avoided the donkey and the leg-breaking journey down. When we returned at sunset to the boat, there was Mel, unscathed and content. What did she do all day? The same thing she usually does. Be Mel. Just lie around like a lizard on a rock. Meanwhile I was like a mad chimp hearing the next day's itinerary, and off I went into the casino, with my people.

The next week we went to a mosque. Mel had decided to join this day; maybe she even had a little cabin fever. As we entered the doors, Barbara wrapped herself up in a homemade burka, and I looked at my own attire. Baby T with no bra. Corduroy bell-bottoms and wacky platforms. Barbara and I made eye contact, and I could tell she thought I was a disrespectful idiot.

I learned later that it had said on the day's itinerary that the women should cover up. I treated that paper each morning like a wasteful tree killer, and failed to learn about the dress code. So Mel, who dressed like she was going to a mosque in everyday life, managed to cover herself in a passable way. I wrapped my back-pack across my front and took off my shoes and found odds and ends in my bag to make do.

As we went in, I started to cheer up because I love prayer. And here I was in a faraway land, doing something I love in an amazing place. I was a student of the universe asking for guidance in how to live, whether for the day or for life.

Everything had fallen away, and yet when I opened my eyes I saw Barbara looking at me in my tiny T-shirt that showed skin as I bowed down. God. I was a nightmare for this woman. And a nightmare to this house of worship. I couldn't take it. Just when I was feeling at one with the celestial plains, I realized that I was just someone else's idea of hell.

We left the mosque and returned to the boat. Mel and I man-aged many giggles, but I was starting to really get depressed. For weeks this went on: Wake up. Eat together. Get on a bus together. Learn together. No Mel. No break in the steps of the day's pro-ceedings. And I was too young and stupid to take in the land. In-stead I was stewing in the formality of every moment being accounted for. It just wasn't me! I was a free bird caged! It was coming to a boiling point.

One day, the boat had docked off the coast and just allowed

people to flow freely or simply relax at the pool. I don't know why, but it was a "snow day" on the Mediterranean for this overly organized group. I walked around, and instead of feeling free, I felt like this boat being stuck out in the water was my final straw. I could see land but not get to it, and promenading around the floating jail was not my idea of leisure.

As Mel tells it, she and Barb were sunning by the pool when a boatman walked up to her with a pained and nervous face. They looked up from their books. "Um, excuse me, ma'am," he said to Barb, "I'm so sorry to disturb you, but your friend has jumped off the boat!" She looked at him, confused, as if he was saying the impossible in another language. "Your friend has jumped off the boat and swum out to that little island, I'm afraid." Clearly this had never happened. Barbara just went red. Mel of course made a hilarious joke—how would they retrieve me? "We will pull down one of the boats and go and get her, I suppose. I am sorry, this is unprecedented." He looked apologetically at Barb.

And it was true. I was on the top floor of this giant ocean liner and something took over me. You know when you start to psych yourself up? I was like, I could make that jump, I could. It's not high enough to kill me. I saw a very small island of just a giant rock out in the distance . . . I could swim that far, right? The height. The distance. The idea was too tempting, and with my heart pounding, double-daring me, it crescendoed into me putting one leg onto the railing, climbing, then the other leg, and then I was at the top of the railing and just said "FUCK IT" and flung myself over a good hundred feet or so and plunged so deep into the water that I struggled to get up to the surface.

But I did! And with that first gasp I broke through and felt alive! The rebel was back! I immediately started off to the rock in the distance, and after about thirty minutes of swimming I reached it. Panting and gasping, I pulled myself out of the water, and I felt like, as much as I was about to die, I also never had felt so alive!!!!! Hhhhhhaaaaaaaaaahhhahaaaaaaaaa, you old fuckers!!!! Look who's the bad girl now!

They all looked at me like I was the jezebel of the ship anyway. The tart that gambles and hangs with the locals and dresses like a whore from 1972! Well, now I have proved you right! Ha!

After the high wore off, in about five minutes, I realized I could not exactly set up camp and live permanently on this inhospitable rock. These people were my ride home. I slumped in defeat because I would have to return with my tail between my legs, and just then, I saw a dinghy in the distance making its way to me. I was half relieved, half terrified of facing Barbara. Maybe she was right. Maybe I was just a misguided, stupid juvenile jerk who had made a series of mistakes in my life.

One of the reasons I was eager to join this trip in the first place was that I had just married a guy I was dating, and I was also trying to help him with all his green card business. The whole thing was a bust, and as good as my intentions were, he was a wreck and I was an idiot, and we immediately shook hands and filed for divorce. At nineteen I had ruined the sacred nature of marriage. I had killed my career by twelve. I needed a major reboot and I had ideas, yet not a total grasp on how to do it.

I was still strangely wearing the cheap band on my finger that was a temporary wedding ring. That night at sunset, as the boat was setting sail once again, I went up to the top deck and looked out at the water. I was a humble ant in the middle of the world, and I had so much to learn. I slipped the ring off my finger and realized and remembered that you can pray anywhere, and so I did.

As the boat started to reach deeper waters, I told the beautiful, colorful sky that I wanted to learn from its all-knowingness! And that even though I was lost, I vowed to do whatever it took to find my way! I apologized for screwing up marriage already and for everything else I might have botched, but I vowed that I was no lost cause! I was worth it for this powerful Almighty not to give up on! Don't give up on me! The pink-orange sky sent me a breeze, and I threw the ring out, and it bodysurfed its way into the deep blue sea.

When I returned to the dining hall that night, much to my surprise, the guests thought it was hilarious that I had jumped ship, and instead of turning up their noses or their backs on me, they asked me many questions about my escapade. All of a sudden, I was being let in rather than rejected. Even if they're amused more than anything, I'll take it, I thought, and with that I finally had something to talk about with everyone. My stint AWOL gave us common ground, and it was the best night on the ship.

I know even Barbara was relieved that I was a hit! I think she unpuckered for five minutes and actually felt good about my presence. Like, "I know! She's always been a little wild!" and "You know, since she was seven she has always done things in her own way," etc. We ate dinner, and Mel and I made our way to our cabin. I put on my mellow blues mix, and as the soulful song "In the Pines" by Leadbelly came on, we talked about cutting our losses and leaving early. I loved the idea of leaving on a high note. And the next day was the day we finally got to the pyramids, so as long as I saw that, I was happy to cut bait on this bitch and go home!

As we pulled into Egypt, I entered the bus practically high-fiving the old-timers, but Mel and I were secretly plotting our escape. We got on the hotel phone and made our reservations to get out of Dodge super early the next day. The boat would be continuing on, but we felt our three weeks was enough.

After completing what felt like a James Bond mission to get ourselves out of Egypt later that night (after the bus trip to the pyramids), we had time to kill, so we put the television on. We turned the dial on the TV and came across a Richard Pryor movie in Arabic. It wasn't *Stir Crazy* or one of the ones I knew well. It seemed to be about him and his family and their "new house." That was all I could make of it before the phone rang and it was the chipper guide to summon us to the bus. I hung up, grabbed my backpack, and said to Mel, "OK, let's go see these pyramids we just traveled weeks to see!!!!" She was lying on her back—one arm under her head, lounge lizard position on the bed—and without looking up at me, she said, "I'm gonna stay in the room." I looked at her with big eyes and mouth agape. "What? It's the pyramids! This is a once-in-a-lifetime opportunity! Are you nuts?" I mean, I knew she was, but c'mon!

She looked at me and pointed her arm and finger. "I can see them out the window." I shook my head. Indeed you could see them out the window as we were clearly in the adjacent-to-the-Sphinx hotel specifically built for tourists. "Wow. OK. I'm out"—and with that I left Mel to watch her Richard Pryor movie in a language she did not speak.

Later that night, when I returned from staring at those pyramids and savoring my newfound lease on life, Mel and I made our way to the airport. It was honestly terrifying being two girls traveling through alone, with all the men and their machine guns. At the airport, they were examining my boom box and were convinced it was some type of detonator. I begged and pleaded with them not to confiscate it. After being threatened, I backed down. But eventually they gave it back. We waited as the men with machine guns looked at us like aliens. Our plane finally came in. It was a Lufthansa flight! We ran onto the flight and sank into our seats, and I immediately downed my complimentary champagne.

As the cabin crew watched us once again, I thought, *Judge me all you want, just take me home, please.*

The good news is we have all grown up a lot. Barb was there, front and center, when I got married a few years ago. I hope she no longer hates me. One day I will be on a trip with one of Olive and Frankie's friends, and I can only hope they don't do to me what I did to Barb.

First kiss

DEAR OLIVE

You are very smart. I know that according to the book *Nur-tureShock* I am not supposed to tell you that you are smart, but you are very sharp. Let's call it that. I have ready many books and studied many things because I always have wanted to attack parenting in a very smart way myself. I'm an overachiever in most areas of my life. I take on a lot and I expect perfection in myself. I am hard on myself. And I'm sure some of that comes from fear. And I admit I was scared when you came into the world because I just wanted to make sure everything was perfect for you. It all started with your nursery, which is French magazine ready, and my approach to making sure everything was perfect was very dialed in, from your supplies, to asking my sister-in-law for the right babysitters, to making sure the birth plan was all taken care of, complete with hospital room, the best doctors, and your grand-parents there and ready.

But you didn't come. You were late. And I waited, day after day. I should have known then that you would be teaching me incredible life lessons from the moment you were born. My birth plan? Not your plan. OK. Got it. You didn't even want to be the astrological sign you were supposed to be and waited nine days and skipped right on into your Libra nest.

Those first few days in the hospital, I thought I would die from fear. Your weight was dropping, we were not sleeping, and I was ill. Dizzy and completely spun out. I brought you home (the first drive was cliché-worthy, surreal and fun), and when I brought you into this perfect room I built for you with your father, it was as if no one else in the world was there. It was just you and me and my concern with keeping you alive.

This did not go away for the first three months. I wanted to control everything. Make every bath the most amazing soundtracked event that ever existed. (I think you are more musical for it, and you love to dance, so that's good.) I was up for days on end. Eating and sleeping were just difficult because I was concerned about your sleep training and getting your bottle down and making sure you burped and that your room was dark and don't get me started on the temperature of the room. I would stand at the thermostat and tinker all day. I became like a bad sketch in a comedy show that wasn't even funny but more a study in the decline of one's sanity.

I showed you everything and explained everything. Red truck.

Yellow duck. The cow says moo. You could count to ten by the time you were one and a half. And up to twenty by two years. It was amazing. You could name over thirty animals and spell and write your own name on your second birthday. You know how to communicate what you want. We have incredible conversations too. You are not in turmoil because you can't truly express yourself. (You flip out because you want more *Peppa Pig* like every other kid.)

You have always known what you needed, and funnily enough you didn't need my worry. In many ways, though not purposely, I took a survivor approach. Not having a model and just wanting to make sure you had consistency and classes and stimulation was important. Most of all I wanted you to feel safe.

I also tried to make you laugh all the time, and you are a semi-serious bird. You like it when you like it. Sometimes "seriously?" is the look on your face, and other times I melt you. You break and crack a smile and say, "Silly Mommy." Come to think of it, there is almost a semipatronizing quality to it, as if you know I am being a total goof. But I can't help it. I like to pander for laughs. It was even my job for a while. I am also a silly person when it comes right down to it. You take things very seriously, and again, for being only two and a half, I cannot believe the things you say or the capacity of your comprehension of a situation. I am already contending with a developed mind.

I can't wait for you to get into school. I want you to go all the way. I will do whatever I can to foster your journey, and I am glad to say that being an overachiever will serve you well. I know you like having so much knowledge at your disposal and you use it well.

You are still a kid and love to watch *Cinderella* five times over, and you love a playdate, but even your art you take very seriously. It's great to watch, and we give you your supplies and watch you go. It's wonderful. It's also great to watch you read so much and say each page out loud and recite the books front to back and even say the authors' names! It kind of freaks me out.

But then again, I have no reference. I have no siblings and no real idea what the normal child-development rate is. You just seem strong to me. Even when you get hurt, you don't want anyone to console you, and you don't want to be held. You want to fix it all by yourself. But of course I want to take care of you. I try to follow your rhythms too. You are very self-aware. And at the end of the day you need my strength and not my worry. You like it when I am very capable and know exactly what to do (this took me a while, but I'm feeling much better now).

I work with Seedlings Group and Safe Kids, both of whom have taught me so much. And I found a book called *Raising Lions*, which helped me find my strength as well. I am the parent. Period. I know I will have to keep researching and learning and experiencing things to be prepared for each new phase. But I feel ahead of it now instead of behind it. I look forward to it, actually. I got this one, and you can always count on me. I promise.

I love being your mom and figuring out what you need. Even if what you need is your independence sometimes and for me not to dance around the room. But I will not stop. I will just have my instincts sharp and ready to know what the moment requires and have a large arsenal from which to pull.

I am so relieved that you are big and strong now. You're not a tiny fragile baby. But you are still my cub, and I will protect you like a fierce bear. We are both growing together in very different ways. And I am so proud of you. You have aced a lot of milestones already, and we are just swimming upstream together, holding hands—well, holding hands when you want to, because sometimes you just want to do it by yourself without my constant hugs and kisses all over you. I can't help it.

I love you in the way where you discover the most selfless true love that one can experience. You are the keeper of my heart. The love of my life. You are trying to just figure it all out right now, but the truth is, I can't wait till you will just collapse in my arms and stay for a while. Like forever.

Poinsettia Place, 1980

THE SEAGULL

I am the Seagull. That's my nickname. I stare at other people's plates with jealousy and curiosity. My eyes are like lasers on a target to everyone's food and this is why: When I was at grade school, at about seven years old, my mother kind of forgot to pack my lunches sometimes because she didn't realize that she needed to. I was fed at work too, so this was just an honest mistake and oversight. Someone else usually took care of it. Like when I was in preschool through second grade, at Fountain Day School, they provided meals. Hot and cold. They had macaroni and cheese, canned beets, and black olives you could put on each finger and then make funny hand gestures with and then eat them one by one off your fingers. Lunch was a happy time where each kid got food and we sat at long lunch tables. It was in a shaded area under a roof, and there was a cool breeze. It was so pleasant. There was harmony and order. And everyone got the same thing, so there was no coveting or competition. We wore uniforms too, so again, even playing field for everyone.

Fountain Day School was a very quaint little school in West Hollywood, and was owned by a nice woman who lived above the property. I liked it there. I felt safe. It was my first experience in school, so I didn't have anything to compare it to. They had a little swimming pool, and little swim meets. They would pick one girl and one boy to be the king and queen every year, which was weird. They would ride up and down the length of the pool on blow-up swans. It definitely was a taste in jealousy for girls. It not only hit the Pavlovian princess fetish, but you got to ride a swan! I don't know what it did for boys, but I do know that our school environment affects so much of how we develop. It provides our first social experiences in life, and they are more than formative. Some are everlasting.

Cut to the new format at the Country School in Sherman Oaks in the valley. This was a dog-eat-dog world. Older kids. No uniforms, and kids were defined by their clothes. They were ruthless toward each other. This was the beginning of cliques too, so you knew your place on the food chain very fast.

Speaking of food, the lunch area was like the Chicago Stock Exchange. When the bell rang, the insanity began. Lunches were commodities packed by parents, so there was a total hierarchy on who had a nicer presentation or who had better content. Peter has a Ding Dong, and Rachel has a Capri Sun. Let the bidding begin.

It was total chaos as each kid sized each other's lunch up, and it became important if someone had a lunch box or a brown bag. (Brown bag was amateur and spit on; a lunch box was like driving up in a Ferrari.) Some parents put their kids' lunches together with care. And some parents threw shit together like their hair was on fire.

But it was all blood sport at these lunch tables, and the major game was "trade." For example, Jacob would turn to Peter and say, "Peter, I'll give you my peanut butter sandwich and some chips in a Ziploc for your Ding Dong?" Peter would look at the kid as if to say, "In your dreams, you Ziploc-toting piece of shit. If you had a brand-name bag of chips we might have a deal, but as for today, keep drooling."

It was unappetizing and terrifying. And unfortunately, since my mom was not used to providing meals, I was not in a good bargaining position most of the time. I had nothing to barter with, and I would stare at these kids' lunches because they had something and I didn't. It bothered me less that I had an absentee father than it did that I was not in the lunch game.

As I sat there, watching all these kids eat and trade and work their sick magic on one another, it reached a fever pitch in my life and truly affected me. I became the Seagull. Staring eyes. Hungry. Darwinian. Too prideful to beg and yet I had to develop a swoop-in approach to get anything. I would suss out my prey and sidle up. "Oh, Peter, it looks like you're not finishing that Ding Dong, can I have it?" or "Sammy, I noticed you have a turkey sandwich—

you know, I've never tasted turkey before." Sammy would just look at me like "I don't give a shit." But I would survive.

Each day I took a different tactic with a different kid, and I got my scraps. Don't worry. It built character. It was a power struggle I suppose we were meant to have. Everyone knew what their leverage was that day. Some days, when a kid would unwrap an aluminum triangle and reveal a piece of last night's pizza, he might as well have produced the Hope Diamond. Everyone would race over and start bidding. Mayhem all over again. Of course, that kid would either reap half the goodies from the entire group, or he would just sit there and eat it, exaggerating each bite and taunting the other kids. As he masticated that slice, the other kids would slowly go crazy with jealousy at the lunch tables. Heads would explode.

And this sick ritual would start all over again the next day. Day after day for years. I am sure this is where whoever wrote *The Hunger Games* got the idea. I should look up if she went to Country School.

And I will say that, years later, at every meal, even if I have food in front of me, I watch what everyone else has. The other day at breakfast this lady ordered the smoked salmon I had contemplated before going with the eggs and sausage instead. When her plate came, I could hear the music start to rise in my head and feel my eyes zeroing in on her plate. It looked so good. Goddammit!

I turned to my husband, and before I could even speak, he knew exactly what I was up to. It's as if I become Lou Ferrigno in

The Incredible Hulk and I start bulging up when I covet food and I need to be talked down. I covet to this day, and that's why my friends still call me the Seagull. I have that desperate look in my eyes, and yet it is pointed, not sad.

However, there is good news, and the moral of this for me is that I will assemble my daughter's school lunches with love and detail. I will labor with bento-box-style precision. It is going to be a chance for me to do it the exact way I would have dreamed of when I was a kid. When I became a seagull in the first place. But don't worry, seagulls are no chumps. And neither am I.

Texas, 1996

TODDETTE

y partner Nancy and I had always talked about driving across the country. We'd always said to each other, "We have to go on a road trip, and we have to go in an RV." We had fantasies of one of us driving while the other scrapbooked at the table! Sleeping wherever we damn well pleased! Flipping quarters at desolate intersections somewhere in the great USA and saying, "Should we go right or go left? I don't know! Let's flip the quarter!" This was a fantasy we discussed for a few years . . . until one night in 1996.

I called her up late and said, "You know, we can keep talking about this or we can actually do it. And I say we just go rent an RV in the morning and GO!" And much to my happiness, she said yes, and we did just that! Our plan was to go from Los Angeles to Wolfeboro, New Hampshire, where Nan's family had a lake house, taking whatever route seemed fun in the moment. We would be on the open road for one month—let the games begin!

We packed our bags, my dogs, cameras, notebooks, and anything else we needed. On our first night we were driving through Palm Springs, and at a checkout stand at the grocery store we heard the checkout lady say to the customer in front of us, "You gonna go see the meteor shower in the monument tonight?" We quickly found out the monument was Joshua Tree!!! We parked our wonderful RV, which we called the Tioga, after the name of the model. We let the dogs go roam, and we climbed up the stairs on the back—the ones where, when you're driving behind an RV on the freeway, you think, why are there stairs back there? We lay down on the roof on our backs and stared up at the sky. I took out my old camera and went with a long, long, long open exposure, and waited for something to happen. To this day I have never seen anything like this: All of a sudden, it started to rain stars as if the sky had turned into a shower and the universe was giving us a cleansing from the heavens above! Not bad for night one.

Next we went through White Sands National Monument; Fredericksburg, Texas; all along the southern coast of the country. And a few weeks in we decided, "New Orleans!" I had never been, so why not!

Had we thought it out, we probably wouldn't have rolled in to the outskirts of town in the middle of the night, but being a stupid girl in my early twenties, I just didn't think of dangers like that. And so I decided to pull the RV into the gas station and fill her up. Nan was somewhere in the back; the dogs were sleeping on the bed; it was a typical night in our weeks-long routine. Until the crushing sound—CCCCCCCRRRRRRRAAAAAAAASSSSSS HHHHHHHHHHCCCCCCCCCRRRRRRRRR- RUUUUUUUUUUUUUNNNNNNNNNNCCCCCCCCCH- HHHHHHHHHHSSSSSSSSSSSSSSSSSCCCCCCCCRRRRRAAAA AAPPPPPPPPPPPPEEEEEEEEEEEEEEEEEEEEEEEEEEEEEEE EEEEEEEE—of ripping metal. I looked up in shock as I realized that I had underestimated the height of the gas station roof over the pumps and lodged myself under it as our RV ripped through the metal overhang!

Oops.

After the loud thunder there was a moment of silence, and I do mean a moment. And then all of a sudden, we heard a shrieking, squawking voice coming out of the glass cashier box. It was distorted due to the fact that the woman was screaming through an old microphone!

Crackling, clucking shrills filled the air! She was yelling words so fast at such a high pitch that I couldn't understand what she was saying. I wondered why she wasn't coming out of there as I moved through the RV to the side door and checked on everyone's status. Everyone was fine. No one was remotely hurt. This was just awkward! SQUAWK SQUAWK SQUAWK!!!!!!!!! The lady screamed again. But why wasn't she getting out?

I opened the side door, and then I saw her. She looked like a cartoon. A very large woman who apparently could not move and refused to try. Crazy wiry black hair and drugstore makeup. She just sat on her tuffet in the glass box, screaming her piece, and her piece finally became clear through the muffled chaos: "I'M CALLING THE COPS!!! THEY'RE ON THEIR WAY!!!!!!!! DON'T EVEN THINK ABOUT LEAVING HEEEEEEEEEEEEEEEERE!!!!!!!!!!!!!!

Shit. OK. No problem. I finally got a look from the right perspective at the damage, and the situation was this: Our roof and the overhang had simply become one. They were cats cradled together, and it wasn't clear how you could untangle it, so to speak. As Nan and I looked around, we started to take in our surroundings in all directions . . . Dark alleys. Trash cans on fire! I think there was possibly tumbleweed! It was clear that we were in one seriously rough neighborhood. I started to panic. It wasn't even the roof that had me shaken up anymore. I started to wonder if the woman in the box couldn't lift herself up or if she knew that leaving that glass box wasn't safe. Shit! I was scared. And just then a figure started coming toward us out of the shadows.

He slinked toward us, going from backlit silhouette to even stranger stringy person with dainty wrists and greasy long hair, as he started to come into focus. The person looked like a he but in some form of drag—negligee slip, flip-flops—but the most important detail on top of this pipe cleaner of a man was that he was wearing pearls. Perfect. As this creature sauntered over to us, he uttered his first words, and they came out in a long flowing southern drawl: "Y'all better get the fuck out."

As we stood there, wondering if he was friend or foe, threat or our latest ally, he looked us straight down the barrel of our eyes. "You ladies really better get the fuck out," and he started moving his hands like an airplane conductor on the tarmac, insinuating we birds needed to fly away.

SQUAWK SQUAWK, the woman continued to shout over the entire exchange.

"Um, yeah, we're stuck," I said, and he looked at me with a calm, knowing look. He didn't have to say, "Yes, stupid girl, I see that." Instead he went straight to the bottom line: "The cops aren't gonna help! The cops are the ones you should fear!" I took in this information. "Oh God," I muttered. Now I was really flipping out!

Nan was in the RV making sure all our business was in order. License, registration, etc.—she was a practical person, getting everything organized and perfect, and I was the one outside crumbling! In the darkness the trash cans were on fire as if someone had turned them up. The whole scene was starting to turn into the Michael Jackson "Thriller" video! Figures were coming out of the cracks and from behind abandoned buildings. I ran back to the RV! "Nan, we have got to get this fucking thing unlodged!!! He says we're in danger, but I think that's becoming glaringly obvious!"

I ran to the driver's seat and hopped in. I poked my head out of the window and said to the mysterious person, "If I try to get myself out from under this, can you help?" He nodded as if I was finally starting to wise up. I asked him my next frantic question. "What's your name?"

He looked at me and said, with a Blanche DuBois delivery . . . "Toddette."

Of course.

Nan and Toddette each took a place outside, her in the front of the RV, him in the back. I could see her out of the windshield and him in the side mirror. The dogs were still hanging out on the bed, staring at me. I pulled the gear down and started to slowly put my foot on the gas. Meanwhile the woman's squawks again turned into "DON'T YOU EVEN THINK ABOUT MOVING!!! I CALLED THE COPS, THEY'RE ON THEIR WAY, ARRHHHH-HHHHHHHHH!" The RV didn't move. So I applied a little more pressure, Nan guiding me from the front like a beacon of all things sane and Toddette nodding small nods over and over! Nothing! No movement. "THE COPS ARE COMING!!!!!" she screamed again! My heart was pounding. I wasn't going to flee the cops; I just wanted to not be stuck when they got there. According to Toddette, this was crucial—"You better get the fuck out"—as if the clock was ticking and the zombies were coming!!!!! According to the surroundings, being a sitting duck was a fool's choice! "OK!" I said to myself. "I have to stab it!!! Floor it! Anything!!!!! Watch out!!!"

I jammed the gas, the RV finally lurched forward, and I flew out in a flash. I heard a giant rip and I looked in the rearview mirror just in time to see, as if in slow motion, the entire air-conditioning system fly off the top and over the back and onto the concrete in a perfect rainbow-arching crash. I then saw Nan and Toddette run to it, each take a side, and crab-walk it to the side door and into the belly of the RV, where there was now a giant gaping hole in the ceiling. It was surreal to see Toddette in the living room of our mobile home. Comforting in a strange way. This strung-out drag queen had become some kind of guardian angel. With his simple wisdom, I did get the fuck out and it was the first sigh of relief I had had in the last thirty minutes!!!!!

After a minute the woman in the box realized that we weren't running away and she took it down half an octave, and we had a minute for small talk with Toddette. Eventually the cops did come; I wondered what had taken them so long, and then I realized that, despite this woman in the box screaming her lungs out for an hour straight, around these parts this is probably not a high-priority case for these officers. Two idiots stuck in a gas station must be small potatoes compared to some of the calls these guys were getting. I noticed Toddette starting to recoil and shuffle slowly backward when the cops arrived. I started to feel so sad. Had he just seen too much? Had he been discriminated against so hard? What abuse had led him to these parts and this life? He went from my new hero to someone I wanted to rescue.

The cops took our information down and referred us to a place that could fix our RV. As they were driving away, I turned to Toddette and said, "Is there anything you need? Is there anything I can do?" Nan came up with some cold hard cash and handed it to him. Again, she is so smart. Toddette wouldn't have benefitted from my crisis hotline style of care. He could use money for whatever it was he needed; I shudder to think. "Well, thank you truly, Toddette. You really helped us out of a jam." I heard the engine turn over, and once again, practical Nan was getting a move on.

I walked to the RV and looked back and saw him slink into the night. In his lace slip and flip-flops. Who knows, maybe he would buy more pearls????

Days later, somewhere in Tennessee, we needed to have some money wired to us from Western Union—let's just say Cajun Campers had cleaned us out in repair bills for fixing the hole in the roof. When we were asked at a pay phone what name to put the money order under, Nan and I both looked at each other and, without missing a beat, said in unison, "Toddette."

Ballet class, 1982

KLUTZ

Aaaaaaarrrrrggghhhhh. I just poured an entire bottle of water all over the counter because I missed the cup somehow. I fell down the stairs this morning. Yesterday my new stroller (which is apparently back-heavy) fell over. Luckily my daughter Olive was walking next to me; her weight would have stabilized it, but it happened walking out of this restaurant where everyone was staring at me—I was so embarrassed. I looked back and they were all baffled. I knock everything over. I trip. I fall. I tear. I spill. I break. Why? Will I ever grow into a graceful person, or will I always be the lame duck who is in a rush? I also find myself apologizing every two seconds. "Oh God, sorry" or "Excuse me" or quickly recovering: "That didn't hurt," "I'm OK," "Are you OK?" When I step on people's feet or walk into people, where is my head, let alone my eyes? Will life always be this way?????????????

When I was seven years old, I went on *The Tonight Show* for the first time, and when I walked out to go up on the stage, I slipped and totally ate it. I think that was the first time I recall feeling humiliated. People said it was cute. But inside I knew I simply couldn't put one foot in front of the other as well as I should. But I had no idea that I would endure a lifelong incapacity to ever be cool.

When I was in the school yard, there was no denying that I simply didn't possess any ability for agility either, as I was always last to be picked for a sporty game. I understood. And although it made me look like a loser, I actually agreed with those team captains. You don't want me!!!!

My mother put me in all kinds of lessons when I was a kid. Piano—I wasn't musical. Tennis—nope, not an athlete. Ballet— don't get me started. That is a cruel world for girls, it's a cliché and tough, and I hated it. I was short, with boobs and no grace, so yeah, I wasn't delusional about my nonstarter career as a ballerina. Like I said, the only budding happening to me was in my chest. Karate was fun and strangely the one thing I really loved. I loved that the boys in the class didn't make me feel bad about myself. They were just as tough on me and I loved hitting back. Sparring. Getting higher belts of new colors. In karate I was getting somewhere. And I didn't dread getting out of the car to go. I had a skip in my step. I liked fighting. I liked being tough.

Then my mother forced me to go to dance class. OK. This was the ultimate screw job. The teacher, Julie O'Connell, and the Julie

O'Connell dancers, as we would now be referred to, were required to wear spandex unitards—it was 1984, and so those were common back then. Doesn't mean it looked good. And she actually made jackets that said "The Julie O'Connell Dancers" on the back. They were disco-rific, satin with gold writing, and if there was one souvenir I could have from those years, it would be that jacket! (If anyone ever comes across it, please find me!)

But in that class, Julie would simply have no problem comparing the girls as we danced around and learned routines. It was as if we were being pitted against each other. And later in life, I would become so protective of girls having each other's backs, and I think it's due to some of these experiences. Schools and youth can be a time when everyone is getting their sea legs. Girls learn they have to stick together, but I don't think that lesson comes without painful youth isolation.

Anyway, there were always these girls who were more graceful. More capable, physically speaking. Better looking in unitards. Period. I was stumpy and clumsy. I didn't have the moves. And the only one I did well at was kicking and punching. That would actually come in handy later—I just didn't know it at the time. Thank you, *Charlie's Angels!* And one day I would be a CoverGirl. And then own my own beauty business. But again, we just don't know what the future is when we are young. I have grown past some things, but I do know that I have never shed my klutziness.

Every day there will be an incident. Every day there will be some humiliation. Every day there will be damage to something or someone, just hopefully not too bad. I think it stems from a bit of stupidity too, I have to admit. When I am trying to balance and carry something at the same time, that is not smart, and it will cause me to spill or trip or drop something. When I am trying to reach that plate high up on the top shelf, what do I expect? When I am trying to multitask, let's say walking as I put the shoe on rather than sitting down and dealing, yes, I might eat it! If I am rushing the zipper, I might get some skin. If I am talking on the phone while running around my bathroom, trying to get out of the house like a mad chicken, I might break something! When does it change? Do I need to become a calm, slow, mature, clear-headed charm school graduate and simplify my whole life? Is this even possible?

Interestingly enough, I now dance voluntarily at the same studio as the one I was forced to as a kid. I am now a willing woman at my fun, sweaty hip-hop hipster dance class, and I finally feel good. I dance with complete abandon. I own it. The whole silly package. It's true when they say "Just wait twenty years and it will all be better!" It was a long time to wait, but actually they were right.

Preteen

GERMANY

I haven't thought about this in so long, but even so, it haunts me daily.

When I was eleven years old I went to Munich to make a made-for-TV movie slash Christmas special called *Babes in Toyland*—a sort of live-action Mother Goose–type of story that had a large cast, including a young up-and-coming Keanu Reeves—and we were there for many months, around four or five. We shot on the Bavarian soundstages where they made such films as *Das Boot*, and we lived near Schwabing, which was a lively shopping district and beer garden area. I really have no idea how or why I was given such a long leash, but I could go anywhere I wanted by myself, and I loved it.

In the film lots of people in animal costumes were needed, so they hired a bunch of American teenagers from the local army base they could get for reasonable money, and it was the kids' summer break, so it worked out for everybody. I was thrilled to be around a bunch of teenagers who knew what it was like to move around and live an unorthodox life. It was 1986, and heavy metal was alive and well, and it was the sound track to that summer. Songs by bands like Van Halen, Ratt, and Judas Priest were the ones that color my memories. We would all make each other mixtapes and share music.

When I wasn't working, I would go to the areas where people could do two things: hang out and drink. For some reason it was very easy to get alcohol whenever and wherever we needed it. I think the drinking age was eighteen and some of the kids were sixteen, and it just all kind of came out in the wash.

And that's what we did: sit around, get drunk, and listen to heavy metal. But one night, a rock band came through the hotel. They were on tour, and somehow I made friends with someone, and sure enough, we got to go see their concert. It was so much fun, and after, of course, in another night of drinking kids, we ran through the hotel once we got back and decided it would be funny to pull off of the doors all the hanging laundry bags that were full of clothes with labeled forms that listed how many pairs of socks (2) and how many T-shirts (3), and we proceeded to run down the hall yelling with these bags.

In an effort to take this crazy stunt higher, we found a bunch of open doors as people were partying in the hotel, and we threw the clothes off the balconies. There was a tiny river below as well, so some of these people's clothes went straight into the water and who knows where from there, but gone most likely. Other garments just lay on the grass and rocks below.

But we kept going, and hungry for more anarchy, I turned to the other kids and said, "Let's go to the floor below and see what's there!" And we all ran downstairs like we were in the *Warriors* movie. And sure enough, there was another buffet of plastic bags with threaded yarn handles hanging from the knobs of more rooms. We grabbed everything in a blind, crazy fury and went back upstairs and started throwing again. All of a sudden I pulled out a pair of sandals, and I threw one, and then this sick feeling rushed over me and I asked myself, what will this person wear on their feet?—as if clothes were disposable but footwear was too far.

My conscience went up in flames, and I retreated and started watching everyone from the back of the room as if I was watching this all on TV instead of being a culprit and instigator. I felt sick. I knew immediately this was so wrong and I hated myself. I don't remember what I did after that, but soon I was back in my room, still in the process of having a talking-to with myself, and I swore that I would never fuck anyone over like that again.

This haunts me not only because I will never forgive myself or chalk it up to drunk, on-the-loose eleven-year-old behavior, but also because, to this day, my clothes have a tendency to just disappear. I kid you not, if I fall in love with an old T-shirt from the flea market, I can guarantee you it will be gone in a few weeks, or months at best. All of my clothes get up, grow legs, and disappear one by one.

Every one of my friends has deemed my closet "Poltergeist" because clothes go in and then disappear. My one friend Kent said that I should tie tennis balls, like in the movie, to all my clothes so that I can pull them out again when they go missing.

During my time of making two babies, nothing fit for three years, so to make room in my closet I put everything in storage, four to five giant moving boxes full of clothes. I went in a few weeks ago to pull it all out because I am sort of finally back to my normal self, pending a few kangaroo pouches and rolls, and all the boxes were gone. Vanished. I also lost all my clothes in my house five years ago. I am telling you that I cannot keep clothes, and I am convinced it is my karma from that night in Munich. And you know what? I say to myself, OK, you probably deserve it. I really am so sorry and remorseful. And I am positive that what I am wearing while I write this will be gone by the time anyone ever reads it.

India, 2010

INDIA

When I was a child, I had this recurring dream. I believed it took place in India. I just knew it. There was no convincing me otherwise. I was always intimidated by the dream, but I knew the dream had meaning and was not just some silly vision.

The dream goes like this: I am hovering above an everlasting desert landscape of goldish-colored sand. I am gliding over it in my perspective; I am not flying—it is the view from a tiny pearl-colored propeller plane. It's an opalescent vessel that is gently coming in for its landing in the middle of this flat, unending desert. Then the dream cuts to a shot looking at the plane from the side. It is on the ground, and all of a sudden, the door of the airplane opens. The kind that folds down, unrolling open. Then, about ten men in white outfits start coming out of the plane. They are all in white, wearing something like Indian kurta pajamas—long sleeping shirts that go to their knees and light pants underneath. And they have white turbans on as well. They all start in a graceful manner out of the plane, in single file, and they walk to a hole in the ground. The hole is a perfectly cut rectangular hole, about ten feet wide, about twenty feet long. The men gather around the edge of the opening, leaving the top of the rectangle space unoccupied. Then the perspective goes back to the plane and one last man walks out. He is holding a golden urn. And then he too walks over to the open space and stands there with purpose. Then the shot rises gracefully up overhead, glides up and over the men, hovers for a moment, and then plummets straight down into the hole, making the whole image fade to black.

Now, I am not in this dream—everything I described is what I see—and the dream has never changed. What does this mean?? I don't know. I don't specialize in dream analysis. And I didn't want it clinically or haphazardly dissected by some whack job. This was my little dream and I wanted to keep it to myself. I was nervous about the whole death angle, there being a burial-like ritual and an urn. But I also didn't want to say for sure the dream was about death. Truthfully, I was like, one day I am going to go to India and I might die there. But I also knew that my dream would not stop me from going one day.

Years later, I landed in the middle of the night in bustling New Delhi! The sounds, the smells, it was the crazy chaos you would think it was times a thousand! I was thirty-five years old, single, a little lost in life. Flossy had just died. I was to meet a man named

Shantum Seth, who was a friend of a friend, and he was going to take me around to some places and be my guide. The goal was no tourist surface shit. We dove into this wild place. He grabbed my hand, removed my shoes, and looked into my eyes, and down the rabbit hole we went! I had waited for this my whole life.

When I was a teenager, I read all these books on religion and really got into Eastern philosophy. Taoism and Buddhism. Animism. I read everything. I was just a novice trying to grasp ways in which people could maintain the mentality that *we are all one*. There was a desire in me to believe that people have extraordinary destinies and that, after all, most of our heroes in life are human beings. We can have faith in those people, and just as important, we can be heroes too. We all have the capacity to be divine, but that damn ego always lets some people think they are bigger or better than others. However, I think that nature does not choose who is safe or who gets to live. It's an even playing field out there when a tidal wave or an earthquake comes along. On the other hand, I don't want to get bogged down in a defeatist feeling that we are insignificant. I have to believe in an ability to do large things in small ways, or small things in large ways. I was not raised in any pious setting, to say the least. But I love faith. I love that people have it. I love anything that gives purpose or unites us. Without judgment, of course.

So here I was. Shantum took me to several places of worship so that I could experience the different cultures and beliefs right in their very houses, churches, mosques, and temples. One Jain, one Sikh, one Muslim, and one Shiva. They all put me in a space of awe, and I was grateful to really be able to feel what these rooms stored inside them. I sat through several ceremonies and prayer sessions. I would pray. I would listen. We walked through huge boxes of water where one's feet would be cleansed before going in, but the water was covered in flies—Western girl, I had to just get over it and deal!

On foot again in the city, I followed the sounds and sights of what seemed like a groovy old Bollywood movie theater! I have sat in the temples of movie theaters my whole life. I wanted to take Shantum into one of my churches, so I grabbed his hand and we snuck in. It was raw and dusty with rickety old seats, a million miles away from Hollywood stadium seating! As we sat there, in the dark, with all the particles of dust illuminated by the light of the projector, I had a true *Sullivan's Travels* moment!

As far as film is concerned, I truly believe in the movie *Sullivan's Travels*! Its message is of most importance. It's about a filmmaker who makes big comedies, and he feels empty and he wants to make a film of depth and substance. So he decides to go out into the world and seek misery, pain, and suffering so that he can then capture them on film purely and honestly. So the man finds it. He ends up, through mistaken identity, being thrown into a very harsh prison. After being in there awhile, one night, the inmates get the privilege of watching a film. It turns out to be a cartoon. While the inmates are watching, they start laughing. The whole crowd just starts roaring. And as he watches them forget about their problems for just one moment, he sees the power of making people laugh. And this filmmaker has the most extraordinary epiphany! He realizes that there is as much merit in trying to ease people's suffering for a moment as there is in "focusing" on it. To ease someone's pain through a distracting, silly, joyous laugh is his lesson. I know there is suffering, so to escape it for a second is truly powerful. That is one church I am staying loyal to. The Church of Laughing.

We left the theater and continued around the tight alleyways and brightly lit main streets. We ducked into another house of worship. Standing in the church, I turned to Shantum and simply said, "I am afraid." He looked at me. "I'm thirty-five, and I don't exactly know where my life is heading, and I just don't even know what I am looking for."

And he said to me, "There should be no 'I' in what you are saying or thinking or feeling. You have to separate yourself from yourself. You have to realize that 'you' are nothing, and 'we' are all everything." I loved this, and eagerly awaited his next sentence. He looked at me with an easy but true connection and said, "We are all a part of everything. You are the sunshine and the air and a flower in a field. You, and all of us, are in the thread of these clothes. Everything is alive and connected."

It's empowering and humbling, being a lover of animism (to believe all things have a soul). I wanted to feel a part of the universe, but for now, I was excited at this notion here in buzzing, bustling New Delhi. Where life and chanting and cooking and cars and bikes and beautiful chaos were all around!!! Here, in this Shiva temple, they painted my forehead red, and I had a scarf on my head, and I was starting to shed my Western Self. I still didn't know what I believed in, but to believe in anything that makes you go beyond yourself is key. All my studies as a teenager were starting to coalesce. The guru and I had a meal after my teaching and an auspicious trek through the city! And we ate in contentment and ease. Our energies meshed. We had started the day at around two p.m., and at midnight, when our legs were tired, our bellies finally full, and my heart beaming with all the doors this man had opened, we finally said good night.

The next day he took me through Transcendental Meditation. Three hours of eyes closed, with no movement allowed. Traveling in your mind to wherever you want to go. I have to admit for the first hour I was so uncomfortable. I went from eager student to "let me the hell out of this NOW." My legs hurt, my back hurt, I was actually mad. I may have signed up for this, but I wanted out. I don't actually know what kept me in, pride perhaps, but I stuck with it. And as I cursed him for throwing me into something that was too advanced for a valley girl like me, I started to picture myself as a bird. What kind of bird do you want to be? I asked myself. An eagle! Why not? Let's get majestic, I thought. And so I took off. Gliding higher and higher, I started to fly. All of a sudden my legs didn't hurt so much. And I soared above New Delhi. Then India. Then I thought about all the places I wanted to go and everything was endless and full of possibility. I soared over the whole world and looked in on friends—it was amazing. Most important, it taught me that we are anything but tethered. We are capable of going anywhere we want anytime we need. Afterward, I had dinner with Shantum's family and ate his wife's food and played with his two daughters. It was so comforting in his home. I may have wondered where my life was going, but for this moment, life was perfect here in India.

After that, I got on a plane and flew to Bhutan, traveled all through the country for a few weeks, then back to India for a while. When it was time for me to go home, I started the long journey at the airport in Rajasthan. When they called our flight over the loudspeaker, the other passengers and I got up and made our way to the plane outside.

OK, here it goes . . .

I walked out onto the tarmac, and sitting there was a small pearl-colored white propeller plane . . . just like in my dream.

I stopped walking and literally went paralyzed. So this was it. The moment of truth. I looked around. It being the last flight out, the sun was starting to set. And when I say sunset, I'm talking, *golden movie hour*. God time. Nature showing off! It was gold!!!! This was the anticipated scenario I had been wondering about all my life. I took a deep chalky breath and decided to face the great unknown. My knees were wobbly and I felt dizzy. What the hell was I doing?????

The engines roared as we started to take off. The amount of time that had passed had caused the gold of the sun to set to its most perfect pink. Like a cocktail you get on holiday. Blush, or the inside of a seashell . . . It was as picturesque as anything I have ever seen. Of course it's going to be picturesque!! I'm possibly about to die!

We took off.

And as we made our way into the sky, I watched the sun, my eyes burning and my throat hollow. I had palpitations in my heart and was in full-tilt panic. All the meditation in the world was not helping me now. I looked like an animal that knew its unfortunate fate. Wide-eyed! Trembling. I started craning my neck, looking for that bar cart, knowing full well they don't sling cocktails during takeoff. Oh God! I was actually rocking back and forth in my seat. The motion was either going to soothe me or get me dizzier so I could pass out. I was a living promotion for Xanax!

I looked out the window again. I was so struck by the magnificent beauty of the sunset, I sat there, quiet. The silence allowed me to ask myself: What if I did get the chance at life all over again? What would I do differently? What would I keep and what would I leave??? My older self was welcoming my younger self into an early womanhood. This wasn't the death dream it might have seemed like for all those years. It was a rebirth. I realized right then and there that in life you have to make your dreams come true. Even if there are just the ones you have to figure out. I went from terrified to optimistic. The plane leveled out and so did I.

My girls

POST PARDON ME

I am braless, and not in a sexy-activist kind of way but more of a sexless schloomp who justifies to myself that sweatpants are a uniform rather than a cozy private luxury. I am a mother of two girls. Olive is three and Frankie is a year and a half. I am an extremely hands-on overachieving mom, and yet I work too. I am also a wife. None of this is in any order because anyone who has these responsibilities knows that it is a juggling act. I feel even "balancing act" doesn't really explain the circus of trying to do all of these things. I have been in trouble for saying women can't have it all. Things have to give if you really want to raise your kids, because it is all-consuming. It's not that you have to give everything up. That's the great news.

But you can't do everything at the same time. Being a mother is about sacrifice. Putting someone else before you. And that includes one's schedule and work load and play mode and sleep mode and creative-juices mode. Inspiration was really hard to get back after I had my babies because all my thoughts were of them.

I remember after I had Olive, I couldn't even think about work. It made me angry. Work felt like a bad man tempting me to be unfaithful to my kids. Or sometimes I just couldn't take anyone seriously, as if they were crazy to think anything was relevant or important compared to keeping a child alive!!! "Oh really? That has to get done right away? Well, you're an idiot for caring" was my inner dialogue as anyone tried to discuss work with me. I just didn't care anymore. Which was liberating, because I had been a workaholic my whole life! But also scary because I need to make a living to raise my children, and I wondered if I would ever actually *want* to work again! Would the pleasure or the motivation ever return?

I dedicate myself to my kids the majority of the time. So when I take time in my day or week to work, I feel torn. It takes me hours to unplug from the laser focus I have with my kids. Then the guilt comes in—"I should be with them"—and unless I have pulled a five-day marathon with them on my own, I don't ever leave the house without feeling like a total piece of crap! I know that I am not the deadbeat parent I am whipping myself over! I am an in-sanely involved, loving mother! Obsessed with my priorities, al-ways being in the right place. I would do anything and everything with and for my kids.

But sometimes, when I am at the pony park or the bouncy-ball place, there is a little miniature devil on my shoulder after a few days that screams "You have to give an hour or two to work!" and then I feel bad that I totally didn't work hard enough that week because I wanted to make sure that my kids get woken up by me! Get their breakfast from me! Get to their weekly activities in music class and art class with me! It seems like men don't do this to themselves and women are just nuts when it comes to their parenting.

Speaking of men, at some of these mommy-and-me groups I go to, it's like a penis-measuring contest over who is the most involved mother! I swear. And then I start to reject that! I can do that by myself, but I rebel in a group environment. I'd rather sit with the kids at my own house and play with Play-Doh and glitter art and order pancakes from "Olive's store" than feel like I have to compete with anyone. I feel like I don't fit in totally with the overbearing mother crowd, as much as I want to be the world's best mom. And yet I know we're all on the same team to get it right.

The conflict it seemed to reach the loudest hysteria in my head after Frankie, when I went back to work right away. I didn't get to have the standard maternity leave. I went straight back in and did a film, which is the thing I have struggled with most. And I had three-day weekends and I still felt like the world's worst mom, and kind of vowed to really take even more time off acting. I was already only doing one film every year or two. I even took three years off. But here, I had moved the family to London, and I was experiencing postpartum depression for the first time.

I didn't have that with Olive. I had the "everyone is stupid for caring about anything and I don't want to do anything but be with my baby" feeling. But eventually, like in slow motion, sound comes back in and the focus gets clear, and all of a sudden you start putting one foot in front of the other. You get the "Oh my, I actually just got a creative idea." Or "I made a phone call about something." I started getting involved again, although life carries on without you and I had the insecurity of jumping back in and wondering if I had anything to contribute. It took a while—like physical therapy after an accident is what I equated going back to work after a baby to. One step at a time, working toward some kind of recovery, knowing everything might not be the same.

This time with my second baby, I just felt like a failure on every level. I also wasn't just trying to make everything perfect with one kid. I was trying to keep my oldest happy and keep her feeling like number one while there was an invader to her throne crawling around. Was I giving enough to my new baby? How much do I just listen to everyone when they say it's most important to keep the older one happy because the younger one doesn't realize what is happening? Really? Because my Olive is Miss Independent and my little one is a "stage-five clinger" and cries if I even leave the room, which I love because Olive is so strong-willed and wants what she needs only when she needs it, and Frankie wants all the mushy love I have to give. It seems to me like my children both need me equally even if their needs are different. So unless I become a human octopus or divide myself up like a pizza, nothing will get my best. I will just be trying to do everything, but poorly, and filled with anxieties.

And so I continued the film, because I had committed to it; and I gave it my all, but I noticed that my pandering Labrador acting style wasn't there because I wasn't totally there. I was older all of a sudden and it was starting to show up in my performance. I'd done a lot of romantic comedies, which were fun, and then *Grey Gardens*, which was a whole other level of commitment. In *Grey Gardens* I shut out the world for four months in complete and total isolation to truly become this icon, but with where my life was at with a family, I knew that would never be possible again. All of a sudden, in my performance, I felt like I was actually doing something that felt less juvenile and desperate. Not to pooh-pooh what I have done, but there has always been an air of little girl to my work, and all of a sudden I was a woman who could take it or leave it. I was happy that this was different.

The reason I decided to do this in the first place was because my husband, my partner Chris Miller, and my agent Peter Levine all said I should. Three men I love. And the irony is, this was a female movie through and through, but it transcends and touches people because it's a great story about two lifelong best friends. And one is trying to make a baby, and one is dying of cancer. So the whole cycle of life told in this love story between these two women has such poetry and strength that I wanted to be a part of it. When they gave it to me to read, I turned the pages of the script with Frankie in my arms, and Olive in her high chair. I would make breakfast for them and be sobbing as I read one page here and one page there, because it was so moving. I told Peter I didn't even have time to read this—how was I going to do this?

And he and my husband vowed to help make it work, and so here we were. My partner in the film was also a woman I could not respect and admire more, Toni Collette. I think she has given some of the great performances of our generation. She was playing Milly, the woman who gets cancer, and I was playing Jess, the woman trying to get through everything to start her family. I was to be pregnant through much of the movie too, and having just had a baby, that worked out very well.

But much more important, I kept wanting to be a part of this because all the women who are most important in my life have lost someone important to them to cancer. My beloved Nancy lost her mom. My mother-in-law, Coco, lost her mother, who was her hero and best friend. When Coco read the script, she said, "I am so proud of you for doing this," and I felt like a little girl who had done something right. It was the kind of praise that silenced all the demons that plague me.

My personal mantra, strangely enough, comes from *The Simpsons*. There is an episode called "And Maggie Makes Three." In it, all of the family is looking through a photo album, and there are pictures of Marge and Bart and Lisa, and then the kids ask, why are there no pictures of Maggie? And so it tells the story of how when Homer was working at the power plant, he wasn't happy. Every day he worked in an octagonal room looking at an Orwellian plaque that read, "DON'T FORGET: YOU'RE HERE FOR-EVER." And one day when Homer came home he told Marge that he was afraid of his whole life slipping away without his ever getting to live his dream, which was to run a bowling alley.

And so they all squeezed financially and made it work and Homer finally got his dream job! He became so happy that even his hair started to grow back! His life fell into place with his wife and two kids, and then suddenly Marge became pregnant. Now, of course, in order to earn the living his family needed, he had to go back to work at the power plant. And so he did.

But at the end of the episode, the kids say, "Yes, but why are there still no pictures of Maggie in this photo album?" And Homer says it's because he keeps her pictures where he needs them the most, and it cuts back to his office, and they are all taped up in front of him on the plaque for inspiration. But the way he has taped all the pictures of Maggie on the plaque, it has covered some of the words, and it now reads, "DO IT FOR HER," and that is what he now sees every day.

Do it for her. That is it. You show that you love them endlessly. You devote yourself. You sacrifice. You parent also by example. The way you live and the things you achieve and the way you behave will be more evident than trying to convince them of anything. I am a stay-at-home mom some days and a working mom others. But I am always first and foremost a mom. When we mothers worry or guilt-trip ourselves, or try to convince ourselves we will ever be the same after having kids, we are missing the point. Because we won't be the same. I feel like I was born the day my kids were and that my life before was only there to gain wisdom for them. The point is you do your best. Your very best every day. You do it, and you do it for them!

My beloved grandfather

THE ROYAL HAWAIIAN

I first met my grandfather when I was around two years old. His name was Shuni. He and his second wife, Marta, lived in Pennsylvania, where my mother was from. My mother was not born there because she was born in a postwar displaced persons camp in Germany. That was also where Shuni met Marta and left his wife— my grandmother and my mother's mother—to be with her. But, according to what my mom told me, the marriage was over long before that and the camp forced my grandfather to think differently. He wanted to be happy, and so the family immigrated to Pennsylvania when they got out, and then everyone went their separate ways.

My mother's upbringing seemed very dark and bleak. Her mother was not kind and then was bitter from her life not going the way she wanted, and she took it out on everyone around her. I don't even know her name. I met her once, when I was very little, and I recall my mom being so guarded and stiff around her. It was air you could slice with a knife. That is all I remember. One uncomfortable encounter. However, I was so fond of my grandfather. I knew in my bones that he was a good person. Interesting. A great artist. He was a stained glass maker, and he could draw so beautifully. My mother could too—she was amazing. I have never dared to draw. It reminded me of her, and yet I think the skill skipped a generation. But I was glad because it differentiated us, although I wonder if my daughters will have that skill.

It runs in our family for sure because my grandfather John and my great-uncle Lionel were also great artists. John actually tried to be an artist until the family business of acting just swept him up, but he always felt like he didn't get to draw his way to success the way he did onstage. If I see the gift in my girls, I promise to foster it. It is so amazing that someone can put out through their hand what is in their head and make it beautiful at the same time. Sometimes I think I am trying to draw a different picture with my own family in my own way. One where everyone stays in the picture.

Although my grandfather Shuni lived across the country, we all made efforts to see each other. He and Marta would come and stay at our West Hollywood duplex for a week or two.

I remember he took me to Grauman's Chinese Theatre to see my grandfather John Barrymore's hands and feet in the cement with all the other movie stars', except John had put his face in it too, as he was known as "the great profile." I loved that he was different and had really gone for it.

As one grandfather taught me about the other, he also helped with my father. One time when Shuni was staying with us, my father had broken in and destroyed our house. He broke all the dishes and ripped things apart, and much worse is that he had taken the hidden spare key. Not wanting him to be able to have access to our home anytime he felt like taking out his anger, my grandfather volunteered to get it back from him. A meeting was arranged between the two of them. My dad came screeching around the corner to pick him up (where my dad got a car was totally dubious, as he didn't own a home or wear shoes and by no means had a car!), and he pulled up, and we watched my grandfather go out, get into the car, and then it ripped down the street and out of sight.

Hours later the car screeched back into the hood, we all ran to the window, which was louvered glass slats, and we saw my grandfather get out of the car, obviously drunk to indulge my father, and walk up to the house. The car zipped away again at a crazy speed, and when my grandfather walked in, he composed himself, smiled, and, without a word, opened his hand and there was the key.

Our next visit, we went to see them out in Pennsylvania. It was my first time seeing snow. One of the things I loved about my grandfather was that he made life interesting. He would explain where snow came from and how it works. He would tell me the functions and yet nothing lost its poetry.

I think my grandfather made me feel like everything was magical. We played in the snow all day and he gave me Peanut M&M's to give to the squirrels. He looked at me with a glint in his eye. "They love it," he said. And he was right. They went apeshit for them. His backyard seemed like a tiny little white, icy-powdery world where creatures ate candy and everything was safe and beautiful.

I was always calm when I was with him, and so sad when I had to leave him, so I was over the moon when my mom pooled together a little cash from the earnings of making *E.T.* and took us all to Hawaii.

It was the first vacation I'd ever been on. I hadn't yet traveled the world for the *E.T.* press tour because the film had not come out yet. It was 1981 and the last time my life would ever feel simple. We went to the Royal Hawaiian Hotel, which is in Honolulu. The entire hotel is pink, a perfect bubble-gum flamingo pink. Like many girls, I have a Pavlovian response to pink, and I just loved it. It was right on the water and it seemed like paradise; in fact it was my introduction to paradise. When we got off the plane, the hot air and smell of flowers immediately transported us. I knew we were in a different place upon landing. It is so open and airy and I couldn't have loved it more.

We all set up camp and spent our days on the beach, or going to fun kids' things like Hanauma Bay, a snorkeling bay, where there were so many fish that you could hold a stack of saltines under the water and, as they disintegrated in your hands, a bunch of fish would swim up and nibble the crackers right out of your fingers. It was a wild sensation, and I couldn't get enough of it. I went home tired. I wished life was like this and yet I guess that's why it's called vacation.

I didn't sleep well at home. I was stressed and an insomniac. That has always been a big telltale sign for me, even to this day— where do I sleep with peace? Not even in my own bed do I feel that way because of just daily life worries. But every once in a very blue moon, somewhere will envelop me and literally put me into an easy, deep slumber, and those places feel so special to me, and rare, unfortunately. Hawaii was one of those places.

During our days in Hawaii, I loved to walk around the grounds of the hotel. Palm fronds would canopy my journey, and I would find myself going to visit my grandfather in his room. He was always doing something—reading, drawing, writing. He was a thinker. One day I came in and we were talking about the human body, and he was horrified to learn that I didn't know my knee from my ear. I just didn't know how anything functioned or what it was there for.

He looked at me. "Do you know why we breathe? Do you know what bones or muscles are? Do you know how we grow hair and why it's only in certain places?" I looked at him. "No, no, and no." I really didn't. No one had ever explained simple or complex workings of anything, not school or any adult.

So right then and there, he decided to make me a human body

chart. Again, when you can just draw something, you can do any-thing. And while he was doing that, I sat in a chair, enjoying the breeze coming through the window. And then I saw the minibar in the corner and silently crept over to it and opened it. I found a chocolate and looked at him with a pleading look. My mother was a vegetarian health nut and never allowed such things. It was the '70s health-nut hippie movement and she was in it. I am not sure I had ever even had chocolate. I looked at him, he looked at me, and he silently nodded the way he did with the squirrels. He knew it was a treat and that treats in life were good.

I unwrapped it and stared at him. He watched me take a bite as my mind was exploding at the same time. I smiled at him. He smiled at me and then went back to his drawing. I knew he was glad I was experiencing something of pleasure. And in our word-less exchange, I understood so much. He believed people should experience things that make you happy. Maybe that's why he ulti-mately left his wife. She was said to have been very cold and mean. Maybe he knew that life was short and that feeling good was cru-cial. Maybe this didn't come easy to him. Maybe it weighed on him very hard at times that he was not able to stay. But he was someone who could recognize joy. And some people cannot, no matter how hard they try.

We sat there on this lazy day. An older man and a little girl, and there was nothing wrong, no stress, no worries. I remember these moments well. Not just because I loved him and appreciated him so much, but because easy moments are memorable to me. He finessed the drawing and then took me through "anatomy," as he called it and wrote that word at the top. He had drawn a man and a woman, and arrows with descriptions so that I could keep them and use it for any reference. It had so much cool information on it, and it was a simple work of art in itself. I put it in an envelope, and that's where it stayed for the next twenty years.

After that trip, Shuni would come out to Los Angeles again when my mother bought our first house in 1983. Life was extremely different, and I had traveled the world, and my mother was taking me to nightclubs, and I was working nonstop. I was different. I don't feel like I spent much time with him, and I have no idea what my mother's and his relationship was moving forward because we didn't see him really. My mother was very private about her relationship with her family and her life. And I was too young to grasp any of it. I was becoming cynical and I figured nothing lasted at that point in my life. My anger was growing and I was so confused. The days of sitting in a room at the Royal Hawaiian seemed so far away. Life was sweet then. Now it was confusing and inconsistent. I missed him. I wished we could have spent more time together. But I figured there was a reason for it that no one was telling me and I just let the mystery linger. And then one day I got a phone call.

I was now thirteen and living at an institution slash rehab. My mother just wanted someone to deal with me. My anger had taken over and I was out of control, and so in the middle of the night, she took me to a place where I went in and the doors locked behind me. I knew that I was not leaving with her. I had gone in and I was not coming back out. A rat. A roach. Trapped.

So there I lived. For one and a half years. And on one particular day, they said, you have a phone call. They took me to a back office, which was weird. Normally you used the pay phones on the wall across from the nurse's station where they could keep an eye on you. So I already knew something was different—I just had no idea what it could be. I picked up a red phone. I remember it was red as if it was yesterday. A Pac Bell push-button-type table phone. "Hello," I said. They hadn't even told me who was on the line. So I waited. "Hi." I recognized my mother's voice from those two small letters she uttered. "Your grandfather has died."

I didn't respond because I burst into tears. I just sat there crying. I looked around this small fake-wood-paneled office, and I saw a few of my counselors just pretending to be busy with their work so as to give me as much privacy and space as they could in this tiny room. It was respectful, and yet I could also see that they had seen it all. Done it all. They were all from broken families and were ex–drug addicts, some worse. And now they were trying to help kids who just came from crappy circumstances and needed guidance. It was a hard-knocks place. No Hollywood-bullshit beachside rehab, but a psych ward deep in the valley. No one who was here in this building or here in this office had seen a safe or easy life. It was a place where you accepted that and figured out if you were going to make it or not. Period. I was just another fuckup dealing with pain. I kept crying and I kept looking at this red phone that delivered such a blow.

As the years passed, I didn't know how to honor him. I have one picture of him and that's it. It's in a frame and I look at it all the time. I show it to my daughters and tell them all about this wonderful man. I wish I could have had more time with him. He was just so amazing. And the only thing that feels within my control is to have my daughters spend as much time as they can with my husband's parents, who are so important to me, and I fight for time with them. I don't have to, really, they are the most loving grandparents you could ever imagine, but I wonder if they will ever know how much I appreciate them. I know they know to some extent. They know how important family is, more than I do in so many ways. But I hold on to all of it. Because it is such a gift. I finally have a family. And I will never, never, never take it for granted. And in those moments where I miss him, if I want to ever visit Shuni again, I can transport myself back to that room. In that pink hotel, with the lovely breeze and my grandfather drawing me a picture.

Hawaii, 2011

DOOR NUMBER ONE

When I first met Liza, she intimidated me. My best friend Robin introduced us, and I would tag along for lunch with them, but our ages were different so I felt like I didn't totally relate to the conversation. Liza was ten years older than me, with two daughters around the ages of eight and ten. She was married. Mature. But cool. She is a high-powered executive who is behind a lot of movies that get nominated for Academy Awards. She has great taste. She is capable, and when I was twenty-eight years old, she just seemed, well, intimidating. But we had a best friend in common, and so I would go to her house for dinners, and there was a great bohemian crowd, with a chef, and her husband, who you could tell is smart and has a great taste for wines, so I would just hold out my glass and try different wines all night. I wasn't married with kids and still had a long way to go until that was going to take place.

Then, years later, Liza and I did a film that she was producing called *Big Miracle*, a true story about a woman from Greenpeace who set off a chain of events when she tried to save three gray whales in Alaska. The White House, Russia, the oil companies, and global media became involved, and for one moment in time, everyone put down their agendas and actually worked together. It was a very good and compelling story.

So Liza and I got to know each other in a different way. I was now thirty-five and single, just back from India. Swearing off relationships for a while because I knew that I wanted things to be different. As women we know that we have a biological window in which we are forced to ask ourselves, do I want to have a family? I knew that no matter what, unless I made big changes in my life, that was not going to happen in the way I demanded for myself and from myself. If I had grown up at all, I was still young in relationships. A woman in the workplace and yet a kid in love. It was time to reprioritize and sweep the decks. Make way for that big, meaningful, life-changing love.

And Liza and I would sit around and talk about it. When we first got up to Alaska, I was in my "I'm not ready" mode. I would say dismissively, "I just don't know what's going to happen, but I don't even know what I want to happen." I was exhausted by having spent the majority of my life thinking about someone else. And all of a sudden I was solo, working in this snow-globe-like atmosphere out in the middle of Alaska. After I came back from India I was reading books again; I had adopted another dog, Douglas, a nervous mutt with chopstick-like legs but a good snuggler nonetheless; and I had discovered football and was watching it like mad. It's amazing the things you get to do when you are alone. It's actually really fun.

Midway through the film, two months later, I had cooled out on the ice floe we shot on every day, literally, and I found myself saying to Liza, "You know, being single is great! I don't know why we treat it like some disease we are trying to cure with a remedy of 'where is he' because I don't want to know where he is all of a sudden. This is great. I like being alone." She looked at me and smiled. I had really changed my tune since arriving. I was sad and doubtful at first. And now I felt territorial about my space and my life.

The film finished and I had a new sense of self. Something had totally shifted here, in this town of Anchorage, and I was really glad. I knew myself in a whole new way, and I actually felt like a complete person for the first time. Not defined by someone else. When I left Alaska, I would go to dinner now at Liza's with a new sense of belonging. No, I wasn't married with kids yet, but I wasn't a kid anymore either. I would drink wine with Matthew, Liza's husband, and talk to her other guests with a newfound place in the world—was this maturity or maybe a sense of calm I simply had never had before? My life had slowed down and I wasn't being a workaholic, which was very healthy, and I wasn't with a man, so really I only had to examine myself and become truly comfortable without any distractions. I could feel the next big phase coming.

I had met Will Kopelman a few years before, in 2008. We met at a friend's house and he asked for my phone number, which I loved because I felt like men were not doing that anymore. In a confusion of the sexes in the modern world, women were now often the aggressors, which changed the old evolutionary court-ship of thunking the woman on the head and then dragging her back to the cave. Which I was starting to miss because I felt like men thought we didn't want to be pursued anymore—of course, we had come too far, which I appreciate, and I don't want us to take a step back in time, but I was tired of being the one to make it happen. So when a man asked me for my phone number I almost fell off the chair. I was thrilled at the old-fashioned question and I quickly gave it to him. He waited two days to call, of course.

We had a lovely time dating for a few weeks, and we truly had fun. But fun was all it was because we were both not in the right place at the time. So we just drifted back into our lives and that was that. But it was so nice. And getting to know him was a com-plete pleasure. But "timing is everything," and I could not feel more passionate about that universal clock that you cannot control because it knows better than you about when things are supposed to take place. And in this new place in my life—I was sleeping alone for over a year, finding the middle of the bed, and really working on myself—I started to become worried about meeting someone because I was really feeling different than I had ever felt in my life. So strong, and I didn't want anyone to take that away. Someone would have to be the human equivalent of an addition and not a subtraction. Period.

It's ironic that we rush through being "single" as if it's some disease or malady to get rid of or overcome. The truth is, most likely, one day you will meet someone and it will be gone. And once it's gone, it's really gone! Why does no one tell us how important it is to enjoy being single and being by yourself? That time is defining and amazing and nothing to "cure." It is being alone that will actually set you up the best for being with someone else.

Then, one night in 2011, I went out after a function with my business partner Chris Miller, and since we were all dressed up, we decided to go out and have a nightcap. I was trying to get the attention of the bartender when the man in front of me—whose shoulders I could not see past, though I was hovering anyway—turned around, and I immediately started to apologize for being in his space, and I realized it was Will Kopelman. Oh. Hello. I shyly looked down.

Something changed right then and there. Here was this cute nice man who I knew well enough to know he was a good person. The training wheels were off and all of a sudden he didn't look like fun. He looked real. Chris looked at me when he turned around and mouthed "Oh my God" and the feeling in the air was obvious. Will was with his friend Diana, and Chris and Diana quickly did some kind of recon because Chris walked back over a few minutes later and excitedly whispered in my ear, "He's single," and smiled at me and sashayed away. OK, maybe the timing wasn't off anymore?

We went on some dates and they were really fun but comfortable and without games. There was a goodness there and a shocking trajectory where everything was just falling into place. Being my date to my birthday. Meeting the parents. Traveling. My friends liked him, which was everything. When I would bring him to functions of mine, I loved that he was classy and could hold intelligent conversations with people and was consistently wonderful.

I started to panic. What about my newfound sense of self? Would that have to go away? Would sharing a life with someone mean I was no longer my own person but a "we"? How could I stay one of two rather than becoming half of one?

Just like anyone who is about to settle down, I started to examine every little thing. Right around that time I asked Liza if she and Matthew had any Passover plans. I was trying to take Will to a special place to celebrate it, considering his family was in New York. Thankfully she welcomed us right in, and off we went for great wine and a great Seder.

I just loved the feel of their house. It is intimate yet lively. Food cooking, people chatting, familiar faces. I was enveloped by the warmth, which was soothing my pent-up state of having been evaluating how this love with Will could grow and warrant going to the next level. At the age of thirty-six, you don't wait years; you examine the relationship after months so you don't waste years and then find yourself without certain choices. Although I am with men when they want to run away from all the pressure of a woman's biological clock! I get it.

Yet this is biology, and it's the facts, so when you're thinking about being truly serious with someone, it is serious. You will get back to the fun soon enough, I hoped.

Of course when Liza asked how everything was going, in another classic girl cliché, I spilled it. I said we were really thinking about getting serious but "how do you know when and how you should get serious and why does it all feel so serious?" She saw the panic in my eyes. She smiled the most cool and knowing smile and laughed and threw her head back and then looked deep into my eyes. She spoke: "Door number one."

I looked at her, confused. "Excuse me," I asked her. She said, "Everyone wants to overthink and analyze and take all the fun out of it and freak out, but the truth is you pick door number one. You choose the great person in front of you and don't play the game of *Let's Make a Deal* and see what's behind door number two because we are so conditioned to seeing what else is out there."

I said, "I thought you might have been talking about *Let's Make a Deal.*" "That's right," she said. "You are so lucky because he's standing right there." She pointed to him and there he was, my accountable, handsome date, who was once again making lovely conversation with my friends. I turned back to her with pride and calmness. "He is so wonderful. And he is door number one. And I know it. And he's right here."

She smiled and said, "And you know what's behind door number two, of course?" I looked at her with my questioning eyes and she answered, "A donkey and a broken washing machine. So just go. Go and make this work. Will is door number one."

And she was right. I didn't question whether he was "the one." I was trying to figure out how I would go all the way with this man and really create that family I have always dreamed of. What Liza was also saying is that there is no room for looking back. You make a choice to commit and you move forward. You live your life. And you appreciate what you have.

That's it! It's the best advice I ever got. I fell in love. I have two beautiful daughters who are my entire universe and who I live my life for. And if you are lucky enough to get the best opportunity, grab it. Hold on to it. And don't let it go. Otherwise you can get a Kenmore. Or a jackass.

Door number one. Thank you.

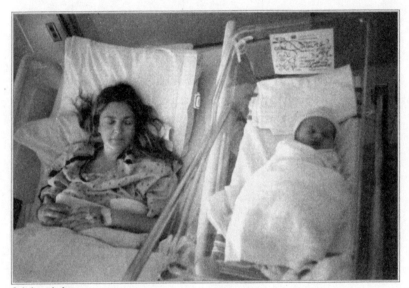

Side by side forever

DEAREST FRANKIE

You are the most delicious little girl, and this is what I have to say about you so far...

When you were born, I had made a playlist for the delivery room. I put Billie Holiday on it and nothing else. It is such soothing music, and when you hear it you are immediately transported to a timeless, relaxing place. (I think that's why so many people put it on during dinner parties, me included.) I knew that calm state of her music was perfect for the mood I wanted to create, and when you were ready to come out into the world, at that very moment, the last song ended, and the next one started. It was "God Bless the Child," and the whole room started to swoon. We all knew that it could not have been more auspicious. What a miracle!

And out you came, and as I lay there, waiting to have you put in my arms, before I could even see you, I heard your father say, "Oh my God, she looks just like you," and of course I waited to see what he meant. You were put in my arms, and I just held you as if I would never let go. We were finally together, and even though I was so woozy, I just clutched you, making sure you were comfortable and looking at your face. Your beautiful little face.

Once we were taken into the recovery room, we stayed side by side for the next four days. Olive came and brought you a present, a little stuffed bear, and watched you intently. As I took a picture of you meeting each other, I thought to myself, Olive, you must look out for Frankie always! I made sure you had each other. It was a sweet visit and Olive was at her best.

Grammy and Poppy came too. Once again, I held up my old camera and took pictures of everyone holding you. We put all those pictures in frames around the house. I make framed pictures for your father for his birthday, and we have a beautiful collection of pictures and moments in varying sizes all around our home. Something I always admired as a kid in the homes I visited. And now we have that too. Even though I had only had Olive about a year and a half before, I had forgotten how everything works, but then it all came back. It's funny how your brain just goes blank, but the training wheels of fear had come off, and I was trusting that all would be OK this time around. Your temperature and your eyesight and hearing tests. I knew you would weigh enough. You were such a good little tiny baby. You never cried or complained. Until it was time to eat. And then you would turn beet red in a matter of two seconds and you would find your war cry! You went from zero to sixty, and for the girl who was so happy and sweet, you wanted that food NOW!!!!!!!!!!!!!!!

And then you would retreat back to sweet, sweet Frankie with a big burp. Which is what I spend my life listening out for, with my ear to your chest, and you were great at it, and it was such a relief to us both. There was never a struggle. You ate like a champ, you slept, and you smiled. Even when you would get a cold, you were nice about it.

And as you grew more and more, you put on your weight, right on track. I would watch your blue eyes get bluer, and your hair get blonder. You fell in love with the bath. You were over the moon to get on solid foods, as if you had been ready since day one. (You got your father's love of food!)

But your smile. Frankie, you have a billion-dollar smile. You light up like a Christmas tree, and you feel it all the way in the depths of your being. You are joyful. Happy. And a stage-five clinger. You start crying if I leave the room. Or put you down. Or have to pass you to someone else. We call you rabbit legs because handing you off is like trying to pass a bunny who simply does not want to be handled. And when you are hurt, you throw your arms forward to immediately intertwine them in my arms and clutch me until you calm down. I love it. I love being of service to you.

I am always trying new foods, spaghetti with tomatoes is your absolute favorite, and you can eat an amount that starts to worry me. I think about all the flavors to bring to you, but I don't obsess on you to learn every color or animal or number. You like to giggle and laugh with me. We both look at the same thing, like you putting sand in your bag of crackers, and you think it's the funniest thing. We both do in that moment. We get each other, and it's more about us sharing a sense of humor. At this point I'd rather have jokes than point out in a book, "This duck is yellow," although you have discovered books and look at them yourself anyway. Somehow I just know you will catch up quick and I don't feel uptight about that because you will have years in school and you are more of a jock at this point anyway.

I am convinced you are a drummer. You even hold your sticks perfectly and will adjust them perfectly if they have slipped. You have rhythm in both arms, and you actually put your whole self into it. It's amazing. (I have already enrolled you in music school. You start in the fall.)

I know that you will grow out of needing to be on my hip or in my arms soon. I can feel it already. You walk and run around and you have things to do and places to go. You will start to find your autonomy, and there is nothing I can do but support you and cheer you on. Somehow this has gone by at the speed of light.

And I don't want you to grow too fast, although I will mark another notch soon on the height chart I have been doing for you and Olive on a wood beam on the wall (the kind I can take and keep if I ever need to—that's why I did it there). You will start to talk and tell me who you are rather than just me projecting that you love smiling as much as I do. You are good at doing your own thing, but I am always right here.

Just don't ever stop needing me. That is what I am here for. You and your sister. To be there every step of the way. I fantasize about the future. And my fantasies are always the same. They are you and your sister feeling like you can always count on me. For the big and the small things, and everything in between. I dread the days you will slam a door in my face (I'm not an idiot, I know what having two teenage girls is going to be like), but I can handle it.

I was built for this. In fact, I look forward to it. I will always do my best to present the high road in life. Teach you to be grateful, polite, and humble. It means everything to me. But you are my teacher too. And so far you have shown me that to love without end is perfectly safe. My heart grew bigger the day you were born, and it grows bigger every time I see your smile.

To say I love you is the understatement of the world. To show that I do for the rest of my life will be my honor and my pleasure. As I sing to you to the tune of "Rubber Duckie" . . . "Little Frankie, you're the one, you always make my day so fun. Little Frankie, I'm awfully fond of you."

Boulder, Utah, 2000

OUTWARD BOUND

N an walked into my office one afternoon in 1998 and said, "Oh my God, they are making *Charlie's Angels* at Sony! We have to pitch ourselves for it." I was in the middle of shoving cheap sushi in my face and she was giving me indigestion. I had been so tightly wound on our last film, *Never Been Kissed*, because vanity deals were dropping like flies, and if your film didn't work you were done for as a production company.

Taking on a giant action movie seemed like enough for me to stop chewing long enough to say with my mouth full, "OK, tell me everything you know." She said the studio wanted to make the movie but that the big idea was mostly what they were working from and they were looking for someone to come in and own it and really make it come alive!

Then she started talking about how she used to play *Charlie's Angels* with her friends growing up. They would all be a different angel and go solve cases. Nan looks like an original cast member, and I could picture it perfectly. And eventually we went in, pitched the movie and the world we wanted to create, the tone, everything. And wouldn't you know it, they took us two gals on.

Then we wanted to hire a first-time director, get a script written with a brilliant writer and create three characters out of nowhere, convince everyone it would be great and to trust us, help in the hiring of all the team of costumes, makeup, and production design to set the look of the world, cast Cameron, find our third angel, Lovely Lucy, call a pay phone to find Bill Murray at a cryptic location and set a time after flying to New York to stalk him in person just to get him to talk on the phone, wrangle the brilliant Crispin Glover and convince the studio to cast an indie darling as the villain, try to combat all the negativity about how much this movie was going to suck from everyone including early press and Internet whispers by writing in the first scene of the film that we know we are making another movie out of an old television show and we are not taking ourselves so seriously so neither should you, keep convincing the studio we would not lose their $100 million investment, crusade for the angels not to use guns but use their brains and hand-to-hand combat instead, train for kung fu, and shoot a five-month-long action film. Then, once it's made, you start working with the team of marketing people and the publicity department trying to figure out how you are going to sell this movie! From the trailers and commercials to posters and a world press tour.

And another way to do that is to do lots and lots of magazine covers. So when *Marie Claire* suggested that the three angels go to Outward Bound because that would make such a great story to publicize the film, we all went for it. But then I found myself being shipped to Boulder, Utah. At that point we had just delivered our first cut of the film to the studio and were getting a whole bunch of notes.

The film was coming out in three months and it was crunch time. We had already been working on it for well over a year and I was burned out and stressed. Instead of being a mature and rational person telling myself that I was lucky to work with all these incredible people and no matter what it's just a movie, I was wondering if all this hard work to have a company was going to crash and burn in a very public and irreversible way. And this company had become so important to me both professionally and personally. I wanted to be back at home problem solving and not anywhere else.

These were my thoughts as we were driving in a van to meet our "instructor," who had a giant hat with the word "BOSS" written on it. I was standing there as he was telling us we would be driven farther out to a deserted space, dropped off, and picked up in three days. We would hike forty miles. We would not have food, sleeping bags, nothing. Just the backpacks we had on our backs. Whhhhhhaaaaaaaaaaaaatttt???? What is happening? Where am I? How the fuck did I get myself into this?

As we continued in the van, I noticed my fellow angels were nowhere near me. My whole vibe sucked, and as I was stewing in the back, I knew they had mutinied to stay away from my toxic energy. Fuck. Cameron and Lucy and I were usually three happy peas in a pod. We loved each other. Learned martial arts together. Laughed together. Pushed and inspired each other. Went to Vegas on weekends together. Braided each other's hair together. And yet here I was, ostracized for my bad attitude. I just kept saying, "How did I get myself into this?" Or "Do I want to sell a movie so bad I'm willing to starve and freeze out in the wilderness for it?" No response. They weren't playing. They were out to enjoy this. Fuck fuck fuck. The van went along driving farther out into where nobody could hear you and nobody cared.

The first night we started hiking and I just kept muttering shit under my breath as I was trailing everyone. Half because I wanted to just be alone, half because my short legs couldn't keep up. I was the least athletic of us three. I could pretend and train to be a badass, but out here there was no faking anything. Shit just got way too real for me and I was pissed. The guide started talking up front about how we would learn to make fire, survive, and find food in these conditions. He started by stopping by a bush and grabbing a hunk of white straw from it, saying, "This is peelu. It's a tree and people use it in toothpaste and gum, but you can chew on it for hours and get water and saliva from it. It's really pleasant. Peelu is your friend. Make a mental picture and let's find some along our route." Go fuck yourself.

We walked for about five miles that night. The terrain looked like dried trees with orange and beige rocks. It looked like the areas you fly over in a plane and think, wow, there's nothing but earth here, and if you were to zoom thousands of miles downwards, you would see us making our way through it like tiny ants.

Once the dark had set in, they walked us over to a flat rock that was about fifteen by fifteen feet, and said, "You can all sleep here tonight." I looked at Mr. Boss Hat and thought, are you out of your fucking mind? And then he proceeded to say, "You will want to huddle together because body warmth is all you have tonight. So the person in the middle is going to get the most heat, but I would rotate all night, it will help."

I was going to fucking murder someone. I knew my dear girlfriends thought I should go suck an egg right now and I knew no one wanted to spoon with me.

But instead Lucy, raising her hand like a good student, said, "They told me that sleeping in the leaves is good too?" And without showing too much pride from her paying attention at our orientation, he said, "That's right. You can gather leaves and make a pile, it makes it a little softer, and you can even use the leaves as a blanket."

Well, I thought, why wouldn't everyone just do that? You stupid ass, why are you suggesting this goddamn rock?

Everyone said good night and dispersed, leaving us to our own devices and to crap in nature, brush teeth, take in the beauty, etc. I just sat there on the rock, mad. I saw Lucy making her leaf bed from the corner of my eye, and I just lay down on the rock, telling myself it was temporary. I decided that I would join her there after she fell asleep and wasn't mad that I was enveloping her from behind. As mad as the girls were at me, I think it was sinking in that this was not easy and shit just got real once again. Nighty-night.

Fat chance. Lucy got up from her leaves, freezing and shivering. "I need heat!" Cameron waved her over, and the three of us relented into our three-way spoon positions. There was no sleep to be had, not one minute. All we did was rotate all night like three human skewers on a hibachi—the only person who wasn't dying was the one in the middle, and when your time was up your time was up.

We barely spoke a word. We just knew what we had to do, and did it. When the sun rose we were happy for some warmth, and we roasted ourselves on that rock for at least a half an hour. I heard crunching footsteps and then the boss guy and his cronies approached. "Good morning! Who's ready to walk twenty miles?" My anger bubbled up all over again. Tired and out of it, we made our way on foot. Again, I was the one bringing up the rear or dragging it down, I'm not sure. Either way I was back to muttering shit under my breath.

I was also so hungry. I hadn't really eaten yesterday traveling, so it felt like two days without food at this point, and it was just another thing to tip my scales of sanity versus insanity. I was lopsided and whacked out. All day long hiking, hiking, hiking, stopping for "life-saving tips" that I absolutely did not listen to. My inner dialogue said, "I would rather die out here" or "Kill me now and do me a favor." And if I ever did get left out in the wilderness again, I probably would die, so there! Take that, boss man.

We started to have to put carabiners on. We were attached to the guides for safety, to make our way down large boulders and rocks into little streams and rivers. We would hold our little backpacks over our heads as we made our way through the neck-high rivers, and sometimes the backpack would make it out dry and sometimes not. But we were truly in the earth now. If our hike last night was a level one or two, this was nine or ten. This was truly being a part of Mother Nature, and we were slithering through her veins like blood.

We got to a large mountaintop and we all started clipping on to our respective people again, men who could give us slack and help us get down if we fell, as we were tethered to them in case of emergency. I didn't even know my guy's name and I am usually the conductor of a group. I am utterly social and usually someone who brings everyone together. In fact my girlfriends knew me as the producer who made shit happen and was in there smoothing everything over when it needed to be. We all did, we were a team, but I was used to being in some kind of leadership position. Now I was just dead weight, a carcass being slowly dropped down a chasm.

Everyone made his or her way down. Lucy did it brilliantly and got lots of cheers and whoops from the group, like "Great job, Lucy, you're like a spider!" and they laughed. Then they yelled,

"OK, now your turn, Cameron!" A born athlete from Long Beach, California, she made her way down like the girl we all know and love. Cool, funny, capable. Everyone roared with delight.

Then came a halfhearted to me "OK, now your turn"—no name, just a "c'mon, let's get this over with and get the unfun one down the rock." And so I did. And while I was clinging for dear life, my foot slipped and I fell a good ten feet, and then I snapped with a hard jerk as my tether caught, and I was just swinging in midair, back and forth like a stupid metronome in unflattering khakis.

"FFFFFFFFFUUUUUUUUUUUUUUUCCCCCCCCCKKK-KKKKKKKKK!" I screamed and then the bat was let out. Wailing as the guy just dropped me down the mountain in midair, one embarrassing foot at a time, I just cried and yelled. And by the time my feet feebly reached the ground my knees buckled and I lay there like a hog-tied loser, all wrapped up in my cords and lines.

A few humble and vulnerable hours later I watched from afar as the whole group bonded. Lucy caught a fish in the river with her bare hands (which she later puked out of her guts), and everyone cooked it and ate it, slapping her back as they feasted. I overheard Cameron saying, "How great was this!" (She later got a parasite called giardia.) Wow. Everyone loved them and their team spirit and can-do attitude.

What was wrong with me? Why was I so at the end of my rope in every single way? I was seething alone in the bushes, furiously eating peelu because no one would officially talk to me.

What was I going through in life? I was twenty-five—was this my midlife crisis? When you start work at basically one, and live life in the fastest lane, maybe this was it.

I had an enormous amount of stress and no ability to filter it in a healthy way. I just would resort back to being a little girl who was never taught how to handle things. But I don't boo-hoo in life. I pick up the pieces when something goes wrong.

I heard myself saying, "Well, once again, you are going to have to figure things out for yourself. You are here in the bushes for a reason and you need an epiphany. And first you need to start eating, licking wounds, and slowly make your way back into everyone's good graces."

I wasn't outward bound but inward spiraling, and I needed to fix this. So I got up and walked over to the nature-loving circle and joined the group. I sat a few feet away, just like when a dog has done something really wrong and it worms its way back in slowly. That was me. The dirty little dog.

That night, I had softened the girls enough to make my way back into the spoon, and we rotated all night. This time we tried the leaves, and it was a little better, but it was all about the human burrito. Simple as that. The next day, we hiked another several miles and made our way to a beautiful river. They told us we could bathe in there later, but first we were going to learn to make fire!

They took us over to a cave to make a day camp where the wind would be milder. They had us take our sticks and twine and make a bow-and-arrow-type thing that would be the tool to make the friction to create the spark to start the fire. Then they explained the kindling—how you go and find something light, wispy, and flammable, and create a little bird's nest with it. You could also take two rocks and rub them together until you create a spark right over your kindling and start your fire that way.

Lucy took the two-rocks approach while Cameron took the bow-friction route. I chose the latter too. Within about thirty minutes they both had fire and were cheered on accordingly. As far as my encouragement from the guides, I had made my way back into the group over the last twelve hours to warrant a token "keep going, you can do it" type of salute. Three backbreaking hours later, I still had no fire. My scraped hand was bleeding, and I was straining out the last of my tears from yesterday, but quietly so no one could see it. I kept saying quietly to myself, "Motherfucker, I will never get this, fuck!"

I kept rubbing, pushing, pulling. I looked like a mad monkey just throwing my arm back and forth, trying to create fire. I would not give up. I was tempted to just turn and say to everyone, "You know what, I tried, and I know you're all disappointed, I just could never accomplish this, so let's just chalk it up to me being the one who doesn't make it out in the wilderness." I could do many other things in life, but this simply wasn't one of them. As I swallowed my defeat and my arm started to slow, I felt sick and ashamed. I was quitting. My arm almost came to a full stop now, just a few disheartened rubs to look like I was doing it rather than actually doing it.

Just then, my inner voice really kicked in, and it sounded different from the one that was practicing my excuses for the last few hours. I heard it, the volume turning up like a dial, fast: *NO! You will not give up! You never give up! It doesn't matter what shit you get yourself in. YOU don't give up!!!!* I started working my arm a little faster with each word of militant encouragement. I was my own personal drill sergeant, saying, *Get up, you fucking loser, and don't be such a loser!* Faster, faster, faster I went, creating a much more momentous friction than before. It wasn't happening. *Still? Why? What's it going to take?* My voice answered me back. *It's going to take everything! Nothing comes easy. Earn it, goddammit!* So I did. I put everything of myself into it and the whole world fell away and all I could hear was the silence of my mind that had been so noisy with negativity the last few days. Now it was clear and I had focus. *I don't care if your hand falls off, you are going to create fire, period!*

I kept going at a furious, physical out-of-body rate. And all of a sudden I heard other voices float in like a wave on the shore: *You're doing it! You're doing it!* I opened my eyes and sure enough! Smoke!!!!!!! I couldn't stop. I kept throwing my arm back and forth on some insane autopilot, looking around with wild eyes. The guys ran over and said with an urgent voice, "OK, now pull back and start to blow on it!" I looked at him, confused, still pushing and pulling, and he said, "If you keep going, it will go out. You have to slow down and get the kindling going and then the smoke will turn into flame." I was so scared to stop, as if it would all fall apart.

But I did. I came to a slow wind-down and started blowing. The guy said, "Slower, less wind, you don't want to blow it out. Slow," and so I whispered my breath onto my little smoking bird's nest and then it happened. It burst into a tiny flame before my very eyes. I looked up, so excited, with wet and apologetic eyes. And my girlfriends looked at me with pride. They knew what I was going through and they just wanted to see me do my best. That's what friends do.

Later that night the guys said they had a special treat for us. And they rolled out three sleeping bags they must have had up their ass because they were produced out of nowhere. Come to think of it, there was a new guy who joined our group that day. Maybe he brought them.

But I was thrilled, and I could never have appreciated it the same way if I hadn't been through what I had been through. Simple as that. Everything has to get taken away. It has in my life too. Everything went away when I was thirteen and I lost my job, my credibility, and my freedom, and I had to rebuild everything.

But like with the fire, I didn't give up. I may not have done it with grace, but I fought my way into something better and more enlightened. I will have many more rounds to go in life. But this was a big one. My lesson here was you do not give up. You hold yourself accountable. You stay grateful. You hold on tight to your friends.

I felt tired and content. The other girls and I went into different areas, as we were all happy to embrace this place independently
for one night after being velcroed together the last two nights. I
slept. A deep and peaceful slumber under the moon and the stars.
I was in my cozy Eddie Bauer sleeping bag, but I slept in Mother
Nature's arms. And when I woke, the three of us met back up, we
were finally alone, and took a long bath in the river. We stripped
right down and took a naked birdbath right there in the wild. It
was a moment, and we all knew it. Mental picture for life.

When we rejoined the group, we hiked for a few miles and
finally returned to the place to be picked back up in the van. I felt
so different than I did when it dropped me off that it was shocking.
But here I was, changed and recharged. I got up in the van and
went to my spot in the back, this time by choice rather than by
rejection. I looked out the window. I heard the voice in my head
come back in one last time, and the tone was different, calm and
kind. It said, "You never give up, and you ask yourself how you got
here? Did you put yourself there? Can you get yourself out? That
was your lesson. Don't forget it."

I won't, I told myself. *I promise I won't.* And I didn't. I went
home, and we made a beautiful success out of the film. And once
again I was simply relieved. But much more important, I had
grown up a little bit more. Right at the point when I needed to.

Africa, 2011

AFRICA

One day in 2004, I was sitting at a coffee shop by myself having breakfast. We were making the film *Fever Pitch*, and it was a really happy time. The Red Sox were winning and about to make history. I was single and enjoying reading the *New York Times* when I came across an article. It said "Children line up to get into classroom," and it was accompanied by a picture of tons of kids neatly lined up in rows, sitting on the floor looking toward the head of the class. These kids had this eager and beautiful look in their eyes. It could not have been more contrary to the look I saw in the classroom in my own experience. These kids fought to be in there. And as I read on it had to do with the fact that the World Food Program was providing meals. My heart broke.

I couldn't have felt more humbled at that moment, and something took over. I was so overwhelmed with empathy and curiosity. I wanted to be transported there right at that moment so that I could better understand the world of this tiny school. Something was moved inside of me to the point where I went home and picked up the phone, only to realize I had no idea who to call.

So I started calling people I worked with. I then was transferred to the UN. When I started my inquiries with them, I was presenting myself more as a volunteer who wanted to learn. Not wanting to take on some celebrity who wanted a photo op was their concern, and I truly appreciated that. I explained that I was allergic to that as well, and this was not that. This was me, just a tiny human trying to educate myself on how their programs functioned. They thanked me for my interest and said they would get back to me. One year later I got the call.

It was actually from *Marie Claire* magazine. They had heard somehow that I was interested in going to Africa, and they had a contact at the UN. If I would write an article about my trip, they would help me get there. They were my liaison and my funding. I had an assignment and I was so excited. I was to take a trip and go directly to Kenya and meet a UN aid worker at the airport. His name was Ben. He was British and immediately had that air of "I hate celebrities." Oh dear. He might as well have said, "Listen, Florence Nightingale, don't try to make it seem like you care because this is a full-time job and not the swoop-in-and-snap-a-picture-and-leave situation." It was similar to when I called. Again I really respected this.

We started right away by going into Kibera, which they called a slum, and it was one of the most densely populated neighbor-hoods in Africa, let alone Nairobi. We went in UN vans with the two UN letters painted on the sides of the cars. Ben said that was to let the people know who we were because the UN was seen as friend, not foe. The UN had no agenda and usually was a symbol of help because if you were thought of as a threat in these parts, you could be killed. Simply put, these were incredibly dangerous places to be, and my first wave of "what am I doing here?" washed over me. There was trash piled up so high that it was the height of a two-story building. Dirty water everywhere. Tiny little store-fronts that were ten by ten feet with a mattress on the floor, and these were what people lived in and worked from. There was a whole world inside of these places, and many people only left to go work at other jobs. The infrastructure, as dire as it was, was very insular. I had never seen such a world.

When we got to the school, the few people running it came out to meet us. We all shook hands and introduced ourselves. But then, a wash of bright colors sailed through my vantage point and the kids started piling out of the small structure to line up. It was obvious that something of a greeting ceremony was choreographed and they were about to perform it. All of the outside world and pain fell away, and the brightness of these kids changed my life forever. It was a Technicolor wake-up call. We spent the whole day with the kids. After their dancing and singing, they took me into the classroom I had fantasized about for the last year. It was shadowy as the only light that came in was from cracks and a few cut-open spaces in the walls. The flags and tiny quilts that the teachers had made by hand on the walls were educational and poetic. There was warmth to this room, and I knew I was in the right place.

I sat in on a lesson and watched these kids practice their English and math. I asked all the kids what they wanted to be. One kid raised her hand. "A pilot." "Really," I said, amazed at her answer. And I said, "You can take everyone to see the whole world." The next one raised his hand. "A doctor." "Wonderful," I said, "you can take care of everybody," and when I said that they laughed. Not a ha-ha laugh but a hopeful laugh. Another kid raised a hand. "A scientist." "Well," I said, "you will solve all the problems." Another laugh.

It astonished me how they were all practical and ambitious occupations. There were no artist or mother or singer aspirations. They wanted to do important things in the world. Again, my heart shifted and grew bigger. At the end of the day they took me to the tiniest closet, which was the kitchen: a wood-burning makeshift stove on the ground with a giant tin pot on it. The pot had porridge in it that also had oil placed in it, and the oil was full of nutrients and vitamins. This was where the World Food Program came in. Ben explained that the kids got one or two cups, depending, one in the morning and one for lunch. It was a red cup made of plastic. Sometimes the kids even saved some of their meals to take home and share with their family.

But without this program many kids had to struggle to get any food at all. It was one of the reasons they came to school. To get an education but to be fed as well. I was acting like I was taking it all in because I didn't want to break down. I thought Ben would have killed me for being a weak starlet who couldn't hack the harsh realities of these surroundings. I just stayed stoic and kept writing things down in my notebook and making notes. I was taking a journalistic approach. After all, I had told the UN I was here to learn. And I would do just that.

After we went home that night, I couldn't sleep because of jet lag and everything I had seen that day. When the morning came, I was eager to go back in to Kibera and learn more. We were now joined by a man from the UN headquarters named Lionello, an Italian man who lived in Geneva and ran the offices. We would be going to a different school that day. This school was more focused on the issues of girls. Rape and genital mutilation were giant problems in this area.

Again, I took out my notepad and asked questions, but inside I was dying. I was feeling in over my head again. I wanted to tackle kids in school, and what I was learning was about the food they fought to eat and the circumstances in which they were living. This was more about how to survive, and the schooling was a great luxury. I was almost catatonic. But I saw Ben looking at me for a reaction and I stayed strong. I was not going to give him the satisfaction of seeing me break like a little bitch. I was among people who dealt with this every day, they were the heroes, and I just wanted to be quiet, respectful, and keep up.

We went through the school, and at this one the kids sang us another greeting song. It was beautiful. When they had started, I was so shaken up again, wondering what I thought I could ever do here. How could I help? I felt out of my league and totally inferior when these kids' voices overtook the self-doubting ones in my head. Their song and joy completely wiped the slate clean, and I told myself, it is about them. If the World Bank could not solve the poverty issues and I could not protect each and every one of them the way I wish I could, because no one could, I could just try to help individual schools. I could try to help these places function one at a time. Maybe even just start with one.

Ben said it was not that simple and the money anyone donates goes into the blanket surplus for all the schools or emergency situations. The UN and the WFP are usually some of the first feet on the ground in crisis situations around the globe. I knew I had definitely found the right place with the WFP; the question was, what was my part in all of this?

I spent the rest of the week there going to several schools in a few areas. Eventually we went far outside the city into rural places. We passed through a huge vista that is an indented crater in the ground as far as the eye can see, and I sat there on the side of the road, marveling at it. The schools outside the city were a complete shift in landscape and facility. A lot of these schools were live-in boarding schools and had actual land. Although it was arid or not as hospitable as you would like, they had a quieter and calmer feeling. Space. The dangers weren't ten feet away. Yet they were no different in what they needed and that they functioned on school lunch programs and donations to stay afloat.

Next I was taken through a few villages of the Masai Mara tribe. This was where I was seeing a part of Africa that looked epic and familiar. They were dressed in bright red plaid that was wrapped around them. They had giant wooden hoop earrings in their lobes, tribal markings on their skin in black and white, and beaded necklaces up to their chins. It was beautiful and incredible.

I was being taken there to learn about where a lot of the traditions come from and to have a better understanding of the way these people lived. They lived in huts that were made by the women. And the men frequented different ones every night. The boys were sent out into the Mara to have warrior quests where they would become men. And the girls had a path that was set for them long ago. Again, this was tradition dating back at least hundreds of years and was not to be questioned, certainly not by me. But I understood how the girls who were able to go to school were getting to have a different way of life indeed. It all seemed a world away out in nature. And yet that's where the girls came from. So it did truly help inform me.

Lionello said we would go to one more place on our way home. It was a hospice for sick children. As soon as we pulled up and got out of the car, this particular little girl started walking by my side. I smiled at her and we kept looking at each other, a sweet cat-and-mouse game of glances. We went into the building and it was a little hospital, but it had actual concrete walls as opposed to mud or wood. It was small and quaint, but it had a really nice feel to it. It was still in a brutal area, but it felt safe, and I was so happy that the kids had a nice place to be, until I realized why they are there. All the kids had different ailments, and I met them and learned about their stories.

The little girl who was following me was now sitting next to me. I watched her. I had been around adults my whole life, and without siblings or cousins, I just didn't have a relationship with little children. In fact I knew they could smell my fear. And then I was a bit undesirable because I just didn't know how to relate to them. Kids are pure instinct as well, and I could tell they could always read my inability to engage.

So I was playing it cool with this wonderful little girl, but then I dared to ask her name. "Edith," they told me, as she only spoke Swahili. But not having to use words probably helped us. And within a few more minutes she was holding my hands. Even when I did try my hardest with kids, they didn't like that I was trying so hard. I just was a failure at being what kids wanted or needed and eventually by my twenties I stopped trying. I just kind of wrote myself off and hung out with the adults. But Edith was giving me the biggest compliment of my life by wanting to be around me.

Not only was I humbled and honored in a way I had never known, I was so grateful for her unspoken bond.

As the day went on, I can honestly say I fell in love. Her calm charm and affection woke something in me that had lain dormant inside since I was a kid not understanding what a kid is. We were like two peas in a pod, giving each other something we both needed. I asked Lionello why she was here. "She has AIDS," he said. "Oh." I nodded. And I held her hand tighter.

When it was time for us to pack up and leave, I was shaking. I didn't want to unlatch from Edith. Unwrapping my fingers from hers was a violation of what we had formed on this life-changing day. I said my good-byes and hugged her over and over. We got in the car, and I waved to her as we pulled away until she wasn't visible anymore. I turned around and looked out the windshield and lost it. I felt so many feelings. Hopeless. Hopeful. Changed. Clear. Convicted. I turned to Lionello. "I want to sponsor her." He asked how I meant and I said, "I don't know, but I need you to help me. I need you to help me set up a trust for her and have the money get directly to her. Can you do that?"

After weeks of hearing how hard it is to get funds to actually make an individual difference and yet how the UN is saving lives with fifty cents a day, I saw there was such a chasm between miracles taking place and there still being too much to do. Somehow starting with her was a way for me to figure out how to give money in a productive way that was so personal and meaningful. I would get to the bigger economic issues once I learned more. Lionello looked at me and said, "We will get it done," and I breathed for the first time since we left that children's hospital. I stared out the window and took in a country I had no idea I would be in one year ago.

I ended my trip having felt like I really experienced different landscapes. We took propeller planes and long rides through the terrain for hours and hours on end. *Marie Claire* even sent me to a safari camp for one night just to say thank you for writing this article. When we returned back to the bustling city of Nairobi, it seemed like a surreal mecca. And yet there was conflict there. I felt confused and yet awake. We all decided, our little crew, to go have a drink that night, as I was departing in the morning.

We recounted the last ten days and asked questions about each other's personal lives; we were getting to know each other a little more. It was nice to decompress for a moment. And that's what amazed me. These UN workers had a great sense of humor. They didn't want to wallow every second. I guess they wouldn't survive if they did. They were matter-of-fact about the problems because they were in it, doing something about it the best they could, instead of cowering at the vastness of it. They seemed like superheroes, and yet they were taking off their masks and having a drink and revealing that they couldn't be more human. And fun humans at that.

The next morning when Ben took me to the airport he seemed

different. Less judging and more relaxed. But when he walked me to the check-in desk he said, "You know when you got here—" I interrupted him: "I know. You hated me." "No," he said, shaking his head and smiling. "I just didn't know if you were full of shit, and it seems like you're not." Phew. Ben was giving his own brand of approval. He even said, "Come back," all of a sudden. I knew that there was a part of him that was also saying, "Because I bet you won't," and I looked at him and smiled now. "I will," I said, with a side of "Watch me, fucker!" And with that we silently dared each other and I left to go to my plane. I wrote my article all the way home as I had ample time and I wanted to write it very fresh off the experience.

After a few days of being home, I was amazed at how much abundance we live in when I entered a grocery store. I got really depressed and felt guilty and totally disoriented. I felt like I couldn't look at anything the same. And yet I had only scratched the surface. What did I know? I knew this was my life out here, but I knew something else now and I couldn't shut it off.

After a few weeks of wandering around, I got proactive and called the UN again—"I'd like to go back, please"—and a few months later I was flying on a return trip. I walked through the airport and saw my greeter. Instead of being shy, I walked right up to Ben and said, "Did ya miss me?" because we didn't need to discuss the fact that I had taken his silent bet and I was back. And this time for a few weeks!

"Let's do this" was my feeling this time, and we went straight into a refugee camp. And as much as I was nervous, I felt like the training wheels were off. There was no one sponsoring this trip, and it was time to go even deeper into the world I had come to care about so much.

The refugee camp was huge. Our bunks were in a fenced-in secured makeshift UN compound, with tiny concrete structures, about ten by ten feet, that each had a single cot and a small wooden table and lamp. That's it, and yet it was very hospitable. Again, in comparison to what other people are living like, it is a great luxury. And you are well aware of every gift you get. We were given dinner, Ethiopian food and a beer. Tusker beer. And we drank one under a tree that had falling bugs. They would cascade right down on your head. The bugs were so large that you would get up out of your folding chair and run at least ten feet, and everyone would laugh at you for getting so scared. But these bugs were the size of small bats, and I couldn't help but flip out, even though they said they were harmless.

I will never forget that night. It was a moment to decompress and yet be accosted by giant raining insects.

The next day we got our start. I was on a tour of schools again, as I wanted to refine my dedication. Schools specifically are what I was passionate about, and they were a contained target. I felt like I could be effective there. It was ironic that I didn't have school as my main priority in my own life, and was so moved by how these kids fought to be here. I would go to different ones and find out what they really needed. What they were lacking. And what it was that was making them thrive.

Some kids had to walk too far, and that made it dangerous or difficult. Villages that didn't have water were a major issue. Schools that had a boarding aspect were more desirable in more desolate parts, and yet in the dense, overcrowded cities the problem was sanitation.

Again, it can get very overwhelming very quickly, but I went around for three weeks really studying what needed to be done. The World Food Program introduced me to an Olympic athlete, Paul Tergat, who was a product of the school feeding program. It was because of the food he was able to train and have the energy to run, and because of the education, he understood what it was going to take to get himself to a place where he could have opportunity. He took me to his original school, and he and I planted a tree there. It was a very happy school with a little bit of land, and the kids were so vibrant and fun. We went to his old house nearby and I met his family.

It was amazing to now be working with someone who was proof of what was possible, and he had important things to say about how it all functions. We moved on to several areas of Kenya. And I fell in love with the village of Kiltamany. I could see that building a borehole here would transform the entire place, and bring water where people had to walk at least five miles a day to fill up a small pitcher. And there was a school, and lots of kids, and it seemed like a wonderful place to build upon. The people were so kind and informative. There was a community. And it affected me and made a lasting impression.

When I was leaving this time, I spoke very seriously to Ben and Lionello about what we could do first. How much it would cost, and what were the priorities. First, it was money to sustain schools in the areas for a year. Then it was helping build these advanced boreholes, which brought water to places in need. Then it was consideration of building my own school and, if so, where.

Again, I had been to so many places at this point—where did I feel a connection to laying down a foundation that could be sustained and monitored? It was a lot to process and I didn't want to just give money and not see where it went, but I also understood that so much money was needed. How could I be most effective?

And when I went back to America, I went to the UN in New York and got my full ambassadorship. I worked with a woman named Bettina, and she and I planned out ways to bring awareness to the program. I got a UN passport, and it was the greatest day. I felt so proud and excited to be part of a place with such meaning and effectiveness. And so I went out touring places on the World Food Program's behalf and tried to get the message out. I wanted to fulfill my position by trying to not just donate my own money but also to get others involved. But I liked my groundwork the most. When I was actually there, and no one knew where I was, that's when I really thrived. I decided to build my school, and I picked Isiolo as the location. I started getting plans and blueprints. I was so excited I couldn't stand it. Things were actually happening and I felt so grateful.

About two years later, when I started dating my husband, Will, who was just my boyfriend at the time, I got a call that the school was ready to be visited. It wasn't fully up and running, but it was ready to make the decisions to finalize it. I had never taken anyone with me on these trips. They were very solo for me and I had yet to share any aspect of this with anyone. But I took a risk and asked Will if he would like to go with me and see it. He said an absolute yes, and off we went, back to Africa. This time I had something to show, and I was very excited to bring him into my world there.

After many days and hours of travel, we went to the site of the school. There were already children there. I played with all the kids and we served lunch. They walked me over to a little painted sign that said "The Barrymore Learning Academy" in hand-painted letters, and the whole thing seemed so real and brought so much joy at that moment I could have burst.

Just then, Will took out his camera and took a picture of me with the kids under the sign. Click. And I knew right then and there that my fears and apprehensions about my energy and how kids perceived it was officially over. Through my learning what they needed, I felt healed of something that had always been painful. A kid who didn't know how to relate to kids. But not anymore.

I could love freely. My heart was as open as it had ever been in my whole life.

Before we left, I made my way to see Edith. She had grown so beautifully. She was taller and healthy. I ran right into her arms and introduced her to Will. We had all met at a park, and her caretaker who was funded by the trust brought her. I spent the afternoon putting my fingers through hers and holding hands with her. I was so happy to be back with her. I was so happy to see how happy she was. And yet there was still that calm in her. But her smile was exactly the same. I am so glad she chose me in this world. I feel lucky. And I can only hope to continue the favor. And this time when we said good-bye I wasn't a total wreck because I knew she would be OK. We hugged for ten minutes straight.

When I went home after this trip, something had shifted inside of me. I thought about getting ready to have my own children. It was time to start learning and investing in what it would mean to become a loving mother. And I knew I was ready. This decade changed me. If I hadn't read that article that day in the diner, my whole life might be different. Or are we set on paths we must go on, and there are little bread crumbs out there to lure us in? I don't know, but I now know a lot more than I did.

And these are the lessons and values I will instill in my girls. They will have to find what it is that's important for them, but I am glad that our house will be so encouraging of that. Every Mother's Day now, I make a Hallmark card for the girls to tell them what I did in their honor. I make donations, or I go and drop off gifts, or we do a volunteer day. It's always for children-related charities. That is what speaks to me. It's what moves me. And until my kids are old enough to figure out what their cause is, I will do it for them, so they get a jump-start on all of it.

It is crucial in my life to do this. I hope I can inspire them. I will do my best. And this is where I put my faith in the rule that kids follow by example. They won't learn a lot from my silly dances. But hopefully I can be of help to push them toward thinking outside of themselves. Africa was my wake-up call. And I am so glad the UN actually took my call.

Arie and Coco

IN-LAW JACKPOT

I walked into the apartment on the Upper East Side for the first time during spring. Will and I had been dating only a few months. It was my maiden voyage into his parents' place, which he lived in as a child. I went from room to room, taking it all in. The art on the walls. Family pictures everywhere, in frames and on the wall. There was a room full of books. A cozy and beautifully appointed kitchen. But I was smitten with the old-school cordless phone from the '80s that remained.

There was undeniable warmth. And all these photographs I kept studying told a story of this close-knit family. One had Will at college with his parents the night of a school play. He and his sister, Jill, in a field of flowers as children. Will as a baby asleep on the beach. Grandparents on their honeymoon. I took them all in, piecing them together like a puzzle to understand my boyfriend's life. Not only was it different from my own—sure, we both had a set of fancy grandparents—but this whole life of "to-getherness captured" was something unfamiliar and frankly intimidating.

I felt my West Hollywood urchin start to kick in. My inner voice, "you don't belong here," and what made it the hardest was attempting to look at his parents. Arie and Coco Kopelman had been married for thirty-nine years with two children, William and Jill, and they had a wonderful life. Good schools for every generation. Great amounts of world travel. Arie was once a "mad men" advertiser and had worked at DDB, one of the biggest agencies in the '60s. He was truly smart and creative, but he had an incredible business sense.

So one day one of his accounts, Chanel, whom he had worked with in advertising for fifteen years, called and said, we want you to come run our company and become president here. They are a family-owned French company and they also joked, where else are they going to find a man with a wife named Coco! It was too perfect. He worked there for twenty years, has since retired, but remains on the board.

Arie had met Coco when she was in college. She was a French girl living in Manhattan, going to Parsons School of Design, and had aced her baccalaureate tests, as she was incredibly intelligent. Smart, stylish, and twenty years old, Coco Franco met Arie Kopelman, and on their first date he took her to the '21' Club in the city. Things went so well that three months later, on her twenty-first birthday, he took her back to the '21' Club and proposed. (Twenty-one is Arie's favorite number.)

So this was what I knew. This is as much as I had learned when Will said his parents wanted to go to dinner and meet me. I had suggested the '21' Club as a fun idea, and they liked it. But I was freaking out inside. Would they like me? Would they be skeptical? Were they cold people even though their apartment would suggest otherwise? Would they look at me and have that "prove it" attitude toward me? I was dating their son, after all.

Somehow this felt like the biggest audition of my life. Although Will and I had been dating only a few months, the girl in me felt the need to become a woman with him. I knew this was different. I had been a "this is who I am" person. All my life I had dug in my heels with men, and all of a sudden I was not fighting for the same things anymore. I could see a life with this man. It was new, but the stakes felt high.

And so I made my way around the corner from the hallway and heard their voices. Will was clearly hugging his mom, and I heard Arie's voice asking a question of some kind. All I know is I was looking down at the ground. My heart was pounding. Most people don't like the parents of their partner. This is a fact. There are movies about it, movies called things like *The In-Laws*, and those movies are about the trials of the family meeting the new girlfriend and then it all goes crazy.

I took a deep breath. My gaze finally started to rise, and before

I could look at their faces, Coco was extending herself and giving me a hug. I saw Arie over her shoulder with a big warm smile. I started to relax my tense body, and turn into a grateful girl who didn't feel judged all of a sudden. Maybe I had judged myself? I was worried about a possible preconception of the "actress girl" Will was bringing home, and that intimidation started to fall away and being my own person kicked in, and I was able to just be myself, which is always the best way to be. But it truly helps when people disarm you. Especially by taking you in their arms.

Off we went for a great double date at the famous '21' Club. The dining room had old model planes hanging from the ceiling and beer steins all around the bar. The space had character and warmth to accompany the tone of the evening. Coco ordered steak Diane, and Arie ordered martinis.

We spoke about our lives and got to know each other. Coco is sophisticated and insanely smart. Sunday–*New York Times*–crossword, graduate-early, speak-several-languages, and know-everything-that-is-happening-on-the-globe smart. Did I mention how amazing her style is? She was also going to be a ballerina, so she truly has grace and poise, but the best part is she laughs hard at a joke. She likes people being who they truly are, and the whole family has an incredible sense of humor.

Arie and I bonded on our love of hearts. I told him I was making a book about them. He collects old Americana art, and a big part of his collection is all things hearts. He also cares about history and preservation. And wouldn't you know it, he is on the board of a whaling museum and I had just done a film about whales and had read thousands of pages on them while stuck up in Alaska by myself for months on end and was so excited to share it with someone. Not everyone wants to talk about the intricacies of whales. But we did.

It was an absolute dream of an evening, and that night I truly fell in love—not just with Will but with his parents too. Affectionate, worldly, humorous, they were everything you could dream of. The strong stability and abundant love of their family unit helped utterly clarify what I was feeling inside that felt a little unknown.

I was thinking about family as well. I wasn't a girl who fancied a boy. I was asking myself the big question of "how will this all function?" and a lot of that is the choices you make. The one thing I swore that I would take seriously was a child. Serious as a heart attack. It was the one thing I would not screw up. I knew I would not even have children ultimately if there was any doubt.

I came from the blueprint of what not to do, and I wouldn't even consider having children until I had the tangible antidote to my experience.

After an old-fashioned meeting of the parents, Will and I took off. We traveled the world for a whole year. The old "how will this function?" question is answered very well with travel. Nancy always says love should be like *The Amazing Race*. She asks, Do you want to be the couple that works as a team or the ones who don't function together? It's true. I used to be late to everything and pack last minute and make going to the airport a nail-biter, and Will finally said, no more. He told me that it gave him too much anxiety.

And so, for the first time, instead of saying my classic "this is who I am," I thought about what that would sound like. "No, I like being a mess who gives everyone an ulcer on travel day, only to potentially miss the flight and ruin the trip." Yeah, that wasn't worth fighting for, so I said OK and started packing the night before.

We went everywhere from Austin to Africa. Hawaii was my favorite trip. We rented a house and cooked and hiked. And for the first time in my life I slept peacefully. We would make trips to New York to hang out with his family. I met Jill, his sister, and her three kids, Sadie, Ivy, and Fletcher—each kid completely different but all awesome. They are fearless, and Jill promotes their autonomy like no one else.

Jill was like a revelation. When I met her, I couldn't believe my eyes or ears. If Morticia Addams got blended with Oscar Wilde with a dash of Lucille Ball, then that would half describe Jill. She is brassy, bold, and intelligent. She is the woman at the table having everyone wide-eyed but laughing hysterically at the things she has the nerve to say. And you love it. But she is also incredibly thoughtful, always has her thank-you cards in ahead of time, and is the person you want to hang out with at the end of the day. Again, I fell in love.

Will and Jill were planning Arie and Coco's fortieth anniversary surprise party in Idaho, where the family has gone every Christmas since Arie and Coco met. This was the big one, and on December 26, the evening took place, and I was just watching in awe. In this intimate room of about forty people who have all known this family since the beginning, Will and Jill read a poem they wrote for their parents out loud that was the greatest and funniest thing you have ever heard.

And in this warm little room, with close friends and family, the snow fell outside. And as we drove home I got a funny feeling. When we were inside, I brought out the candle for the night, as I had brought a travel menorah. It was the seventh night of Chanukah, and to honor Will, who is Jewish, I wanted to provide a way to celebrate his religion. We lit the candle and said thank-yous for this incredible night.

We were as warm in our hearts as the candle we held, and I felt almost dizzy with the amount of love and goodness I had just witnessed. Will said he would be right back, and I didn't watch what he was doing. I just stared at the burning flames. Just then I felt a total rush. I turned around as Will was on his knee, with a ring box.

Oh my God. I have no idea what we both said in that moment, but all I do know is that we had both fought to get here. And although our paths looked clearly different, somehow we had found our way to this love. And we knew that we wanted to build on that love. And so I said yes, and three weeks later, I found out I was pregnant.

Of course, we told Arie and Coco first. I was so excited to be having a child in these people's world that I knew I was off to the right start to do everything different. This safe, unbreakable family was getting a new member and I just felt so lucky. We all decided to have the wedding in June, when I would be six months pregnant. I loved the idea that our child would be able to attend!

And as we were planning the wedding, I called Arie. "Hello, Arie," I said. "Oh, Drew," and he yelled for Coco to get on the line. This is what they always do when one of their kids calls. I pictured Coco picking up the 1980s cordless to join the call. "Hi, guys," I said. "We have been planning along, and I wanted to ask you both a question." They said of course. "Coco, I was wondering if you wanted to walk down the aisle with Will so that we could all walk together? And Arie, I was wondering if you would give me away?" He took a second. "Oh wow," he said. "Are you sure?" "Of course! There isn't any other way I can picture it." He said yes, and we did.

On the day, when the four of us were getting ready to walk down the aisle together, I looked around. Sadie, Ivy, and Fletcher were flower girls and boy, Jill was getting ready to read a passage from *The Velveteen Rabbit*, and I looked over and saw Coco. I saw that she was truly happy. She was wiping a tear as she was kissing Will, and all I could think was that I have to always make her feel that he is happy too. I love her and respect her to no end. I thought,

I hope to be a mother in any way like Coco. She is my idol as a woman. She took Will's arm. We walked down the aisle, and when I reached the chuppah, Arie lifted my veil and kissed my cheek. Little-girl fantasy check! My dream had come true.

My husband that night made a great speech, and all the Kopelmans' lifelong friends were there, which I felt was important, and all my friends, who were my original family, were there. Jill made the best speech ever and had everyone howling of course, and most important, Olive was there. Our daughter, who we hadn't met yet but who was about to be the apple of her grandparents' eye.

When Olive was born, Arie turned to me and said with his classic Arie whole-face smile, "There's nothing overrated about being a grandparent," and he means it. Olive and her cousins have the best grandparents one could ever imagine. He said the same thing when Frankie, our second daughter, was born. They were there for both births, and held each girl hours after they were born.

And when I would watch them holding their granddaughters, all bundled up, fresh and new after their long journey in my body, I would thank God for Will's parents. I couldn't love them more. And for the first time, I am part of a family. In the lottery of life, I hit the in-law jackpot. The really big one.

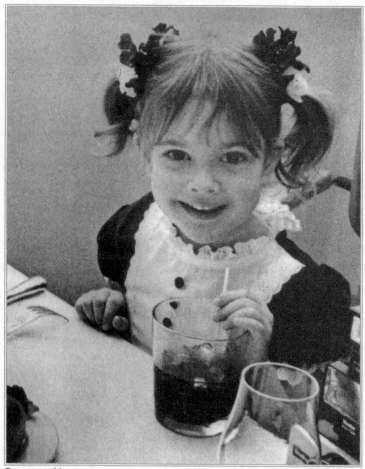

Four years old or young

ALL-AGES PARTY

I never know anyone's age. I cannot tell if someone is thirty or fifty. I can't tell if you are twenty-three or thirty-three. And I have no idea with kids. Babies I can now nail because I am a mom who has gone through three years of stages, so I can tell in a second how old your little one is to the week.

But the reason I don't know age is because one valuable lesson my mother taught me was that age didn't matter. And therefore I was taught not to pay attention. She would speak emphatically about people being mature or immature, but it never had anything to do with a number. She said that young people might be beyond their years and someone older might be childlike. She never asked anyone his or her age, and she lied about hers. I had to sneak in once when she was showering and go into her purse and pull out her driver's license like a thief and look at the age. Then, when I confronted her, she told me that it wasn't true because they had to make up a birth certificate for her because she was born in a displaced persons camp in Germany and thus she had no real birth certificate. Therefore the driver's license wasn't accurate. Then I would press her again for her real birth date, and she would just look at me with a sly smile as if I was foiled again and saunter out of the room, leaving me confused and not knowing what to believe.

Was she lying? And if so, which part was she lying about? The age? The certificate? I would start to look up German camp years in history, but with no Internet and no encyclopedias at my disposal, I would forget by the time I got to school, and my schools were always hippie messes with no real library.

I guess I could have asked someone, but a seven-year-old asking about a displaced persons camp seemed odd, and I felt vulnerable asking anyone. Who was she? How old was she? How old was I? I didn't feel seven. I felt older. And she was always hanging out with younger people, so maybe age wasn't what it seemed to be anyway. Maybe she was right. In fact all my friends were older because that's where I was in life. When I was a kid, I didn't connect with kids.

Now I love hanging with the kids and I find them so very fascinating. The things my daughter says to me at three are so charming I can't take it. I would much rather talk to her. And I for sure know people who are wise for their age and I know adults who are proverbial children and are totally stifled in life.

So hell. Maybe she's right. Age doesn't matter. I have always celebrated an all-ages party in my work. I want it to be inclusive to all. I have never been concerned with trying to land a certain crowd; I want everyone to feel invited. So come on. Come one, come all. Even if you are one or one hundred. It doesn't matter. In fact it all begins and ends in diapers. If you're lucky.

And for the record, I still don't know my mother's age. I guess it will have to remain a mystery. But age is never my concern. It never will be. It's the person inside the shell that draws me in or doesn't. When all my different employers for all my different endeavors ask me the question "What ages is this for?" I always say the same thing: "Everyone, hopefully," because I want an all-ages party. It's so much more fun!

This year, at my fortieth birthday party, I had a dinner with all my lifelong friends. Some were friends from school, some were mentors, in-laws, and it was a mixed bag of ages for sure, and yet all these people mean so much to me. But one of the most compelling aspects of the night was the fact that for the first time in my life, I finally felt my age. When I was young, I never got to be a kid. Then, when I was in my teens and twenties, I was aggressively trying to recapture my childhood and finally be carefree the way that I thought kids got to be because I never got that chapter.

Now I feel like a woman. A mom. I own a cheese board! The truth is I still feel like a kid in moments, but I actually feel like I have truly intersected with my number. I am forty. I am really happy. And I am lucky to say that it feels really great!

Acknowledgments

To my Olive, Frankie, and Will Kopelman; Arie and Coco Kopelman; Jill, Harry, Ivy, Sadie, and Fletcher Kargman. The best family in the world. Thank you for letting me crash the party! Thank you for having me at all. I love you so very much. Just read the book and you'll see.

To the Flower team, and my first family, Nancy, Chris, and the great Mason Hughes, who is my rock in every way. You all are what I wish to be like when I grow up. And thank you for never giving up on me as I get there.

Simon Green (literary agent extraordinaire): You were the person I showed almost seven years of writing to, and you kindly made me wait until I was ready. And then you introduced me to Jill Schwartzman.

And Jill Schwartzman (editor extraordinaire): If you are reading this, thank you for allowing me to have my writing read by anyone. You are the maker of my dreams and a dream come true all at the same time.

Steven and Kate ... love you both, and I admire you and learn from you always.

Bryan Lourd, Peter Levine, and Steve Warren. You are the lions that I follow.

A special thank-you to Robin Fredriksz, who always said to me in a playful yet forceful tone that I should write about my stories.

And in no particular order, girls who make me swoon. I am proud and honored to be your friend . . .

Cameron Diaz, Gucci Westman, Aliza Waksal, Lona Vigi, Jesse Lutz, Lorene Scafaria, Melissa Bochco, Crystal Meers, Justine Baddeley, Kim Davis-Wagner and Tamra Davis, Juliet Casablancas, Toni Collette, and Liza Chasin.

Brittany Baird and Jessica Sodd. My partners in helping raise great girls who will one day be great women. Like you two!

Bill and Karen Juvonen. Thank you for making me feel like a daughter! I love you both.

And to Jimmy Fallon. You are the greatest. Go Sox!

To Diego Uchitel for taking the picture on this book's jacket as I jumped up and down like a happy nut. To Ally for helping me with the pictures. You are the keeper of the castle. And thank you to Deb Ferullo and Mr. Daniel for making me presentable always. I love you both.

To Francesca Fuente, whose taste I trust and love. Howard Altman and Gretchen Rush, thank you as well!!!

And to my mother, Ildiko Jaid Barrymore. Thank you. I am ever so pleased to be on this planet!

And to my father, John Drew Barrymore. See you again someday.